OBEDIENCE
The *Joyful* Discipline?

by
Patti Brown

This book is dedicated to all my fellow strugglers on the journey. May we find the joy and the laughter along the way!

OBEDIENCE
The *Joyful* Discipline?

Copyright © Patricia B. Brown—All rights reserved.

First Edition 2021, printed in the USA.

ISBN 978-1-7356046-0-2

Cover art "Garden of Gethsemane" © 2017 by Lance Brown. Cover design by Patti Brown.

All Scripture quotations, unless otherwise indicated, are taken from *The NET Bible*© copyright 1996-2018 by Biblical Studies Press, LLC. All rights reserved.

Excerpts from the following C.S. Lewis books used by permission:

Mere Christianity by C.S. Lewis copyright© C.S. Lewis Pte. Ltd. 1942,1943,1944,1952.

That Hideous Strength by C.S. Lewis copyright© C.S. Lewis Pte. Ltd. 1945.

The Screwtape Letters by C.S. Lewis copyright© C.S. Lewis Pte. Ltd. 1942.

Surprised by Joy by C.S. Lewis copyright© C.S. Lewis Pte. Ltd. 1955.

The Last Battle by C.S. Lewis copyright© C.S. Lewis Pte. Ltd. 1956.

"Church Mice" cartoon © 2021 by Karl Zorowski. Used with permission.

Contents

Acknowledgements	iii
Introduction—The Journey Begins	vii
Chapter 1. Defining Obedience	1
Chapter 2. More Than a Definition	7
Chapter 3. Whom Do You Obey and Why?	25
Chapter 4. How Do You Obey?	33

- Blind Obedience
- Dutiful Obedience
- Trusting Obedience
- Joyful Obedience

Chapter 5. The "D" Word—Discipline	65
Chapter 6. It Isn't Easy (Obstacles to Obedience)	77

- Fear
- Confusion
- Doubt
- Shame
- Pride
- Blame
- Selfishness
- Greed
- Resentment
- Laziness
- Lust
- Grief
- Stubbornness/Rebellion

- Impatience
- Ingratitude

Chapter 7. Warning: God Responds to Disobedience   129

- Discipline
- Abandonment

Chapter 8. The Divine Rewards of Obedience   139

Chapter 9. Heroes of Obedience   153

- Jesus Christ
- Abraham
- Moses
- Daniel
- Peter
- Paul
- Mary
- Zechariah
- Gideon
- Joseph
- Hettie Chappell
- Oseola McCarty
- Your Name Here?

Chapter 10. So, What's Your Problem—Besides That? 161

Acknowledgements

No writing project is every really produced in a vacuum or is the result of a solo effort. I was privileged to learn much from the sermons of three extraordinarily gifted pastors, Rev. Paul Stallsworth, the Rev. Dr. Steve Castle, and Rev. Karl Zorowski. With their permission, I have included with attribution many of the insights I gained from their sermons. (I freely confess to being a detailed note-taker during sermons!)

Looking further back, I doubt my soul would be in the condition it is in today had it not been for the faithful efforts of some other spiritual directors and pastors along the way, some of whom have since left the Church Militant for the Church Triumphant. I thank God for all of them! Fr. Richard Somers, Fr. Bill Henry, Fr. John Vollar, and Fr. Abram Dono—devoted men of God—shepherded me through some of the deepest crises of my life. The gentle wisdom of Rev. Keith Tonkel (who always preferred to be known simply as "Keith") showed me "Jesus with skin on" for the first time when I was only thirteen and visiting a Methodist youth group. Almost two decades later, by God's mysterious Grace, it was Keith who conducted my wedding and, just a few short years after that, pastored me through the horrific aftermath of my father's suicide—one of far too many suicides in my life.

Thank you all for your faithfulness to God, especially as you expressed it in the ministry to which you were called.

I also want to thank my pastor Karl Zorowski and my friends Becky White, Becky Bolduc, Brenda Roberts, and Jeff Bolduc for taking the time to review the draft of this work. Pastor Karl provided priceless theological and textual input (as well as an original "Church Mice" cartoon!). As a former teacher, Becky White's keen editorial eyes proved invaluable. As an artist and a writer, Becky Bolduc was able to view my work from several perspectives. Brenda Roberts gave me the insights of a woman whose life is steeped in prayer. Lt. Col (ret) Jeff Bolduc, who serves as Lay Leader in our church, took time during his recovery from hip surgery to provide many wise and thoughtful suggestions. And although mentioned last, I want to thank my beloved husband Rod— who is always first in my heart—for his patience, his encouragement, his comments, and most of all his love.

To John Rosemond, thank you for your unexpected encouragement, which both surprised and humbled me.

The breathtaking cover art is from a painting by Lance Brown titled *Garden of Gethsemane—Jesus Praying*. Lance graciously licensed its use for this project. And yes, you can purchase prints from his website: paintedchrist.com.

You should understand my convention of referring to God as *He* in this work is because I relate to God as a loving Father, not because I think God is a man (Scripture clearly tells us God is a spirit). If you find father images challenging because of painful experiences in your own life, please don't let my use of the masculine pronoun be a roadblock to your finding this book useful.

Scriptures are quoted by generous permission. All Scripture quotations, unless otherwise indicated, are taken from *The NET Bible©* copyright 1996-2018 by Biblical Studies Press, LLC. All rights reserved.

I offer my undying gratitude to The C.S. Lewis Company for permission to use extracts from the following:
- *Mere Christianity* by C.S. Lewis copyright© C.S. Lewis Pte. Ltd. 1942,1943,1944,1952.
- *That Hideous Strength* by C.S. Lewis copyright© C.S. Lewis Pte. Ltd. 1945.

Acknowledgements

- *The Screwtape Letters* by C.S. Lewis copyright© C.S. Lewis Pte. Ltd. 1942.
- *Surprised by Joy* by C.S. Lewis copyright© C.S. Lewis Pte. Ltd. 1955.
- *The Last Battle* by C.S. Lewis copyright© C.S. Lewis Pte. Ltd. 1956.

I discovered C.S. Lewis the science fiction writer years before I discovered C.S. Lewis the Christian writer. I make an annual practice of re-reading all his works; it's like having an extended armchair visit with an old friend. Of all Lewis' fiction, *The Great Divorce* and *That Hideous Strength* have "spoken" to me the most, each and every time I read them. In the latter, I've always marveled at how Lewis—at the time a bachelor—was able to so accurately understand the perspective of a woman.

Most importantly, I thank God. I thank God for creating me; I thank God for redeeming me through the work of Jesus Christ; I thank God for calling me to a life I could never have imagined. I thank God for never abandoning me to the often daunting challenges I faced, and I thank God for all those "exactly who I needed, when I needed them" companions on my faith journey (especially you, Dolly!).

Introduction—The Journey Begins

Every book has its own genesis or beginning. For me, the question underlying this journey was inspired by the prayer of "Confession and Pardon" in *The United Methodist Hymnal* "Service of Word and Table." The communal prayer reads:

> Merciful God, we confess that we have not loved you with our whole heart.
> We have failed to be an obedient church.
> We have not done Your will, we have broken Your law, we have rebelled against Your love, we have not loved our neighbors, and we have not heard the cry of the needy.
> Forgive us, we pray.
> Free us for joyful obedience, through Jesus Christ our Lord.
> Amen.[1]

Since I am blessed to be part of a local church that celebrates Holy Communion weekly, for hundreds of Wednesday nights I have prayed this prayer aloud as part of the liturgy. Upon reaching the words, "Free us for joyful obedience, through Jesus Christ our Lord," I often wondered, *What is joyful obedience? How can obedience be a joyful thing?* After all, who actually enjoys being obedient?

I had no idea my question was about to be answered when I read Debbie Macomber's "My Spiritual Vocabulary" article in *Guideposts* magazine[2]. She shared how her practice of choosing one word to study for an entire year has impacted her life and career. The concept of doing a year-long study focusing on just one word intrigued me. Since it was already December, I thought I'd try it during the upcoming year. However, rather than select my own word, I decided to ask God's opinion (warning: this can be a dangerous thing!) In prayer I asked, *Lord, what word should I study this year?*

Given my personality, I expected to hear *patience* or *endurance*. I'm very good at doing things with great intensity for a short period of time. I'm definitely a sprinter, not a marathon runner.

To my surprise, the word I heard wasn't anything I expected: *Obedience*. Everything in me protested: *No, no, Lord, surely not that word.* Certain I couldn't have heard correctly, I prayed again in all seriousness and once more asked God for a word to study over the next year. A few seconds of silence followed. Then I heard, *If you want one word to study, then study obedience.* I felt my muscles tense. If there is one word I do not like, it's obedience.

I decided to try God's patience once more. *Are you sure you want me to study obedience this year*? I asked. This time I heard nothing. Feeling a hint of a divine sigh in the silence, I remembered how Keith Tonkel used to say, "If you're wondering why God is silent, ask yourself this: is there something He's already told you to do that you haven't done? Then why should He waste any more time talking to you?" With a sigh of my own, I resigned myself to the project. A year-long word study on obedience it would be, but I was feeling less excited about it by the moment.

My struggle with obedience is a complex thing. In many ways I was not a strong-willed child. I was too afraid of my mother's wrath if I wasn't compliant, and I was often bullied at school. I grew up essentially an only child and that made me independent. Both of my older brothers had graduated and left home by the time I was in grade school. We lived in a small coastal town where I spent most of my free time entertaining myself. I rode my bike, walked on the beach, explored the woods, and read voraciously. What I did not do in all that solitude was develop a very good set of social skills.

Independent, solitude-loving people who by their very nature don't play well with others have difficulty with the concept of obedience. It's not so much an overt rebellion as it is a sense of confusion. We're used to doing what we want, when we want, so we search for creative ways to be able to do it.

I think God has a challenging time reaching people like me. So, too, do many of His followers. I only learned after my conversion experience my sophomore year in college that the Christians on campus had considered me a "hard case" because of my independence. I wasn't particularly interested in what God or others thought. I was what Paul Stallsworth would call a "good pagan." I either followed the rules or found socially acceptable ways around them. I had few vices, was doing quite well academically, and was content with my own company. Not surprisingly, I was also an atheist. I simply saw no need for God.

For me, coming to faith in Christ wasn't about recognizing my need. Or was it? I saw something in the Christians around me I didn't understand and couldn't quantify. There was Alan Jenkins, who had left college a sullen and surly young man and returned radiating pure joy. There was Mary Hart, whose devotion to her God was a wonder to see. I credit her with starting the train of thought that led to my saying "Yes" to God, and to this day she doesn't even remember the conversation that did it! It was simple enough. "You know, if you're right and I'm wrong, then I've lost nothing by what I believe," she began, "because I meet your standards. But if I'm right and you're wrong, you've lost everything because you don't meet mine."

For someone like me whose belief system was above all else expedient, those were curious words. It occurred to me if she was right and I was wrong, I might miss out on something eternally important. I confess that my main thought at the time was to hedge my bets. If I followed her path and it didn't work out, I could always leave it and go back to my path.

One clear, cold winter night I stopped to look up at the stars and found myself thinking about what Mary had said. Suddenly I felt a strong, imperative sense of: *"Choose. Choose NOW."* I also had the odd feeling that whatever choice I made, the other option would be closed to me forever, for reasons I cannot explain. It seemed I was standing on the brink of eternity. Finally, with great candor, I said, "Okay, God. If Mary is right and I'm wrong, and Jesus Christ really is the only way, then I'm Yours. But I warn you, I'm coming with a lot of questions!"

Not exactly a textbook prayer of surrender, was it? In truth, all I did was crack open the shell around my closely guarded heart the tiniest bit. But God is quite gracious and I learned He will not only accept the tiniest invitation, He will welcome it. Something changed that night. No, actually *I* changed that night.

The point of all this is that when I heard the word *Obedience* after I asked God for one word to study for a year, I shouldn't have been surprised. But maybe, just maybe, it was time for me to actually learn something about the subject. And maybe, just maybe, I was ready to learn. What follows is the result of one year spent listening to everything I heard through the filter of one word: *Obedience*—and what happened during the years after. Please note this is not a chronological study as much as it is a dimensional journey of exploration that I now invite you to share.

CHAPTER 1

Defining Obedience

Obedience is a concept. It's also an action. Being both can make obedience challenging, if not difficult, to define.

It's one thing to define an object you can see and touch because the object itself does not change. The pencil you hold today will be a pencil forty years from now. It is something else altogether to define a concept or idea. Concepts can be static, real and solid. A *structure* is something that protects you from the elements, but you can also see it and touch it. Concepts can also be fluid and molded by the culture at large. *Health* is generally agreed to be an absence of illness. While *sick* once meant a lack of health, today it equally means something that's wonderful (as in, "aren't those apps just *sick*?").

We use words to define words. It's important to remember words mean things, but what? Words can describe concepts, but words can't really define them (have there ever been words adequate to define love, for example?). Words can also reflect the cultural meanings that change over time. When Shakespeare's *The Tempest* has Puck laughing about "appearing as a crab in a gossip's bowl", the *gossip* to which he refers was understood in those days to be someone's godmother, with no negative attachment to the word. The word *gossip* only later came to primarily mean any person who was a talebearer.

So how is this relevant to the attempt to define obedience? Consider how *Webster's Third New International Dictionary* defined obedience and its associated forms[3]:

Obedience—1: the act or fact of obeying or the quality or state of being obedient; compliance with that which is required by authority; subjection to rightful restraint; 2a: Jurisdiction, control, rule—now used chiefly of the spiritual authority of the Roman Catholic Church over its members; 4b: a sphere of jurisdiction; an ecclesiastical or sometimes a secular dominion; 3: bow, curtsy; 4a: an official position or specific assigned task or responsibility within a monastic establishment; also the part of such an establishment devoted to the activities of a particular function; 4b: conformity to the rule of a monastic order and to the will of its superior; 4c: a specific and usually written precept or injunction from a superior in a religious order to one of the congregation; 5: a system of dog training designed to develop the intelligent response of the animal to the demands of his handler by means of a graded series of specific problem situations of increasing difficulty.

Obedient—1a: submissive to the restraint, control, or command of authority; willing to obey; 1b: subject, subservient; 2a: conformable or conforming to the control of an indicated agent; 2b: acting in conformance to an indicated situation.

Obey—1: to fit one's conduct to and perform as directed or requested by; 2: to submit to or accord with: a: to rule one's conduct in accordance with; b: to act or react in conformity with.

The reference work I used is quite old, but I selected that particular dictionary for a reason. When *Webster's Third New International Dictionary* was published in 1966, it caused a storm of controversy in the academic world. Yes, with all else controversial going on in the world at that time, a new dictionary did just that. Prior to the publication of this edition, the philosophy behind dictionaries was they served to proscribe language; in other words, they dictated the proper usage of words, implying there existed some reservoir of "proper" language out there somewhere from which to draw. For this reason, editors intentionally left out words considered vulgar or profane. The proscription was so strong a word wasn't considered valid unless you could find it in the dictionary. "Show it to me in Webster's" was a standard challenge heard during Scrabble® matches.

Webster's Third New International Dictionary took a completely different approach to words. Its editors decided a dictionary should reflect *how* language was being used without attempting to control it. Its inclusion of "those" words was a source of horror to school librarians everywhere and was the reason some libraries went years without replacing their old dictionaries. But the impact went deeper than that. The change in philosophy revealed a somewhat shocking truth: there was no reservoir where "authoritative" language resided. Telling students who had spent years struggling to understand the rules on how to use language correctly that there really were no absolutes gave a subtle but insidious permission to overthrow constraints as a whole. I can still remember how I felt when, as a young college freshman, the thought first dawned: if the rules to language weren't based on anything absolute, where perhaps were other supposed rules no long applicable?

Within a decade after *Webster's Third New International Dictionary* was published, the definition of obedience in most dictionaries was simplified to variations of its first option ("compliance with that which is required by authority; subjection to rightful restraint"). Obedience, of which half the earlier definition had to do with religious applications (and not necessarily favorable ones), was now defined simply as an act of submission to authority—this in a culture that had increasingly come to despise and reject any and all authority. Obedience as a concept was disdained and the action of it was certainly not praiseworthy. To be obedient was to be seen as being passive, unable to think for yourself, doing blindly whatever you were told. Is it any wonder why, as our culture has continued to coarsen and crumble, no one cares to talk about or teach obedience as a value to be prized and cultivated? And what people in their right minds would embrace obedience as something in which to rejoice?

Perhaps it's time to reclaim the word obedience. C.S. Lewis, in his preface to *Mere Christianity*, warned how words can become useless to their original meaning if not protected and defended.[4] In one of his sermons, Karl Zorowski pointed out, "When we ask 'what does this word mean?' we usually run to a dictionary for the answer. But the cultural variations can hide the thing. We live in a culture that disdains obedience in part because much of the meaning has been lost. You can't really know it until you do it, until you're tested on it."

What is so wrong with admitting that there are authorities higher or more powerful than ourselves? It's a reality in the workplace. If you are employed by someone else, that person outranks you and tells you what to do. If you are self-employed, your customers by virtue of their wallets hold power over you. It's a reality in society. Drive 85 miles an hour in a 25-mile zone, and the officer who stops and writes you the ticket, the judge who fines you, and the insurance company that raises your rates all outrank you in authority.

You can try to re-define obedience as much as you like, but obedience itself will remain the same. You can substitute all the words you want for obedience, but it won't work. Obedience is a means to an end. It's just not always the end you envisioned. Obedience to the laws of society is necessary for a peaceful society. But obedience to God is a means to something beyond your wildest dreams. Obedience is the gateway to the grand adventure God has planned for you.

And you'll never experience it until you step through and begin to explore it.

CHAPTER 2

More Than a Definition

First and foremost, obedience is a choice. Reduced to its most basic element, obedience is choosing to do what someone wants you to do. You could argue, and make a credible sounding case, that a coerced person has no choice. What you really mean when you say that is, a coerced person has no reasonable choice. In Daniel Chapter 3, Shadrach, Meshach, and Abednego were faced with what appeared to be a "no choice" situation: worship King Nebuchadnezzar's golden statue or be thrown into a fiery furnace to die a horrible death. However, the three young men understood they had a different choice altogether: to obey God or not to obey God.

Let's review the events as related in Chapter 3 of the Book of Daniel:

> King Nebuchadnezzar had a golden statue made. It was ninety feet tall and nine feet wide. He erected it on the plain of Dura in the province of Babylon. Then King Nebuchadnezzar sent out a summons to assemble [the provincial authorities]...They were standing in front of the statue that Nebuchadnezzar had erected. Then the herald made a loud proclamation: "To you, O peoples, nations, and language groups, the following command is given: When you hear the sound of the [musical instruments], you must bow down to the ground and worship the golden statue that King Nebuchadnezzar has erected. Whoever does not bow down and worship will immediately be thrown right into

the middle of a furnace of blazing fire! Therefore, when they all heard the sound of the [musical instruments], all the peoples, nations, and language-groups began bowing down to the ground and worshiping the golden statue that King Nebuchadnezzar had erected.

…At that time certain Chaldeans came forward and brought malicious accusations against the Jews. They said to King Nebuchadnezzar, "…But there are Jewish men whom you appointed over the administration of the province of Babylon—Shadrach, Meshach, and Abednego—and these men have not shown proper respect to you, O king. They don't serve your gods and they don't worship the golden statue that you have erected."

Then Nebuchadnezzar in a fit of rage demanded that they bring Shadrach, Meshach, and Abednego before him. So they brought them before the king. Nebuchadnezzar said to them, "Is it true, Shadrach, Meshach, and Abednego, that you don't serve my gods and that you don't worship the golden statue that I erected? Now if you are ready, when you hear the sound of the [musical instruments], you must bow down and worship the statue I had made. If you don't worship it, you will immediately be thrown into the middle of the furnace of blazing fire. Now, who is that god who can rescue you from my power?" (Daniel 3:1-18)

What a choice! Three young Jewish men, forcibly taken from their land and placed in Babylonian society to be assimilated into that culture, were faced with a seemingly no-win situation: commit idolatry of the worst sort or be burned alive. It becomes quickly apparent Shadrach, Meshach, and Abednego fully understood the nature of the choice offered them.

After their initial disobedience was reported to Nebuchadnezzar, he became enraged but gave them one last chance, in case the report had been incorrect. In an effort to impress upon them the hopelessness of their situation in the face of his power and authority, he taunted, "Now, who is that god who can rescue you from my power?" Their response was, and is, an extraordinary statement of faith:

> "We do not need to give you a reply concerning this. If our God whom we are serving exists, he is able to deliver us from the furnace of blazing fire, and he will deliver us, O king, from your power as well. But if not, let it be known to you, O king, that we don't serve your gods, and we will not worship the golden statue that you have erected." (Daniel 3:16-18)

There was no hesitation, just a clear statement of a well thought out choice. In response to the king's challenge, they recognized and acknowledged their God had the power to suspend the laws of nature and save their lives. But rather than presuming on that confidence, they also acknowledged that God might not choose to do so. Then they took a step farther and said if the latter were the case, it would not change their decision to choose to serve God rather than obey the king. And in this knowledge, secure in their belief, they made their choice and God's breathtaking response to their obedience still resonates today:

Then Nebuchadnezzar was filled with rage, and his disposition changed toward Shadrach, Meshach, and Abednego. He gave orders to heat the furnace seven times hotter than it was normally heated. He ordered strong soldiers in his army to tie up Shadrach, Meshach, and Abednego and to throw them into the furnace of blazing fire…Then King Nebuchadnezzar was startled and quickly got up. He said to his ministers, "Wasn't it three men that we tied up and threw into the fire?" They replied to the king, "For sure, O king." He answered, "But I see four men, untied and walking around in the middle of the fire! No harm has come to them! And the appearance of the fourth is like that of a god!" Then Nebuchadnezzar approached the door of the furnace of blazing fire. He called out, "Shadrach, Meshach, and Abednego, servants of the most high God, come out! Come here!"

Then Shadrach, Meshach, and Abednego came out of the fire. Once the satraps, prefects, governors, and counselors of the king had gathered around, they saw that those men were physically unharmed by the fire. The hair of their heads was not singed, nor were their trousers damaged. Not even the smell of the fire was to be found on them!

Nebuchadnezzar exclaimed, "Blessed be the God of Shadrach, Meshach, and Abednego, who has sent forth his angel and has delivered his servants who trusted in him, ignoring the edict of the king and giving up their bodies rather than serve or worship any god other than their God!…Then Nebuchadnezzar promoted Shadrach, Meshach, and Abednego in the province of Babylon. (Daniel 3:19-30)

When it comes to obeying God, we always have a choice. We may not like the choice. It may not seem, or even be, a reasonable or fair choice as we understand reasonableness or fairness. But we have a choice nonetheless and are therefore without excuse.

****

Not only is obedience an inward attitude (choice), obedience is also an outward action. So too is disobedience. Once the choice has been made—to obey or not to obey—all that remains is the execution of that choice. Bert Herring, a very wise member of our Sunday School class, was fond of saying, "No battle need ever be fought in the flesh that was not first lost in the mind."

Obedience even applies to the inanimate world. Recently I was enjoying an outdoor concert given by a bluegrass trio playing a string bass, a mandolin, and a guitar. I was fascinated by the sounds the musicians could produce from these instruments, and it struck me that it is the nature of the created to obey the purposes of the creator. A stringed instrument is created to produce music. When the strings are plucked, they respond in obedience by their very nature.

In Genesis 1, creation itself obeys the voice of God in coming into being and functioning as it was designed to:

> God said, "Let there be light." And there was light!...God said, "Let the water under the sky be gathered to one place and let dry ground appear." It was so...God said, "Let the land produce vegetation: plants yielding seeds according to their kinds, and fruit trees

> bearing fruit with seed in it according to their kinds." It was so…God said, "Let there be lights in the expanse of the sky to separate the day from the night, and let them be signs to indicate seasons and days and years, and let them serve as lights in the expanse of the sky to give light on earth. It was so." (Genesis 1:3, 9, 11, 14, 15)

True obedience does not exist unless the opportunity for disobedience also exists. When God created man and placed him in the Garden of Eden, God established only one proscription requiring obedience—to refrain from eating from the tree of the knowledge of good and evil:

> The Lord God took the man and placed him in the orchard in Eden to care for and maintain it. Then the Lord God commanded the man, "You may freely eat fruit from every tree of the orchard, but you must not eat from the tree of the knowledge of good and evil, for when you eat from it you will surely die." (Genesis 2:15-17)

This one prohibition is necessary for the man (and later the woman) to demonstrate true obedience. The command to be obedient by not eating of the tree of the knowledge of good and evil was the first lesson in moral discernment and wisdom. God says in effect, "Here is Lesson 1: Obey Me—respect My authority and commands—and live. Disobey Me and die." By choosing to disobey, a person acquires the capacity to discern good from evil, but as a consequence that same person is morally corrupted and rebellious and will no longer consistently choose what is right. Hence the pattern of original sin creates a tension within all of us that Paul and James both described in their letters. As the apostle Paul complained in Romans 7:19, "For I do not do the good I want, but I do the very evil I do not want!" The apostle James stated, "So whoever knows what is good to do and does not do it is guilty of sin." (James 4:17).

I once heard a radio program on which the speaker said the words "You shall die" should more properly be understood to mean, "You will play God, defining good and evil. You will die because when you are God you will kill the very purpose for which you were created—to have communion with God."

In Genesis 3 we see how choice leads to action:

> The Choice:
> Now the serpent was more shrewd than any of the wild animals that the Lord God had made. He said to the woman, "Is it really true that God said, 'You must not eat from any tree of the orchard'"? The woman said to the serpent, "We may eat of the fruit from the trees of the orchard, but concerning the fruit of the tree that is in the middle of the orchard God said, "You must not eat from it, and you must not touch it, or else you will die." The serpent said to the woman, "Surely you will not die, for God knows that when you eat from it your eyes will open and you will be like divine beings who know good and evil." (Genesis 3:1-5)

> The Action:
> When the woman saw that the tree produced fruit that was good for food, was attractive to the eye, and was desirable for making one wise, she took some of its fruit and ate it. She also gave some of it to her husband who was with her, and he ate it. (Genesis 3:6)

The serpent was indeed clever. Eve made one incorrect statement—God did not say "and you must not touch it"—and the serpent exploited it to humanity's undoing. I wonder if Adam, to whom God gave the command before Eve was even created, conveyed it incorrectly to her or if she edited it on her own. Regardless, Eve made a conscious choice to disobey God and the consequences came swiftly.

Karl Zorowski has pointed out that the serpent didn't ask the woman to sin; he merely asked her to think about things differently. The basic premise of temptation that leads to disobedience is, "What if…I do it differently?"

After the confrontation with and denials of our parents, God pronounced judgement upon the woman: the consequences of her sin would produce a conflict/power struggle between man and woman—the woman will want to control the man, but the man will fight back to control the woman. This conflict will continue throughout human society, transcending societies and cultures. James D. Mallory, Jr., MD, in *The Kink and I,* claims the deepest fear of a woman is to be treated as an object by a man and the deepest fear of a man is to be controlled by a woman. He says it is not until Christ that a way out is offered. In Christ man and woman call a truce and live harmoniously.

> For just as through the *disobedience* of the one man many were made sinners, so also through the *obedience* of one man many will be made righteous. [emphasis added] (Romans 5:19)

Obedience may be an action, but those actions can sometimes be silent. In one of his radio broadcasts, Charles Swindoll said silent obedience is the best form of obedience. I thought about that the next time I read Matthew 21:28-31a:

More Than a Definition

> [Jesus asked] "What do you think? A man had two sons. He went to the first and said, 'Son, go and work in the vineyard today.' The boy answered, 'I will not.' But later he had a change of heart and went. The father went to the other son and said the same thing. This boy answered, 'I will, sir,' but did not go. Which of the two did his father's will?" They said, "The first."

Although Jesus' point was about the importance of believing in Him regardless of whether you started young or changed your mind later to get to that point, the parable also says much about the principle of obedience. Both sons are directed by their father to "go and work" in the family business. The first says, "I will not," but then later has a change of heart and obeys his father. The second says, "I will, sir," but does not go. I've never before thought about the silence involved in the first son's obedience.

I'm sure his initially voiced disobedience was anything but silent. Perhaps it was petulant or perhaps it was resentful. Surely his body language, the tone of his voice, the flash in his eyes all communicated his indignation at being asked to do manual labor. Perhaps the family was wealthy and the father's request was unusual. Perhaps the first son was simply selfish about his own desires. Whatever it was, he said "No" and I imagine he didn't say it kindly.

We're not told why this son had a change of heart, but the important point is he chose to obey his father in the end. However, apparently he didn't go back to his father and make a production out of it. He simply obeyed. Silently, he went to work doing what his father asked him to do. I'm sure his father knew about it, though. He either saw the young man doing what had been asked of him or someone else (most likely his servants) told him. Silent obedience makes a powerful statement.

The second son was silently disobedient. Notice how respectful he is: "I will, *sir*." Then he does what he wants to do. Lip service isn't obedience. Obedience is in the action. Jesus had strong words about lip service without action:

> Jesus replied, "If anyone loves me, he will obey my word…The person who does not love me does not obey my word." (John 14:23a, 24a)
>
> Why do you call me "Lord, Lord," and don't do what I tell you? (Luke 6:46)
>
> Not everyone who says to me, "Lord, Lord," will enter into the kingdom of heaven, only the one who does the will of my Father in heaven. (Matthew 7:21)
>
> …but whoever does them [these commands] and teaches others to do so will be called great in the kingdom of heaven. (Matthew 5:19b)

Thinking more about silent obedience, I see how Jesus made a point of praising silent obedience:

> Then he [Jesus] sat down opposite the offering box, and watched the crowd putting coins into it. Many rich people were throwing in large amounts. And a poor widow came and put in two small copper coins, worth less than a penny. He called his disciples and said to them, "I tell you the truth, this poor widow has put more into the offering box than all the others. For they all gave out of their wealth.

> But she, out of her poverty, put in what she
> had to live on, everything she had." (Mark
> 12:41-44)

Jesus also gave a warning to do good deeds in secret, without drawing attention to yourself:

> Be careful about not living righteously merely
> to be seen by people. Otherwise you have no
> reward with your Father in heaven. Thus
> whenever you do charitable giving, do not
> blow a trumpet before you, as the hypocrites
> do in synagogues and on streets so that people
> will praise them. I tell you the truth, they have
> their reward. But when you do your giving, do
> not let your left hand know what your right
> hand is doing, so that your gift may be in
> secret. And your Father, who sees in secret,
> will reward you. (Matthew 6:1-4)

I am often astounded at how many times we Christians ignore Jesus' teaching on this subject. How many ministries make a huge fuss over their larger donors, publishing their names on "honor rolls" or giving them gifts or opportunities to meet the rich and famous at their annual events? I once argued this point with the director of an organization with which I volunteered. She argued back that without recognition, the wealthier people didn't donate. I was unbelievably saddened when I heard that. It seems there is still so much to learn about silent obedience.

****

Scripture tells us obedience is a prerequisite for wisdom. "To obey the Lord is the fundamental principle for wise living; all who carry out his precepts acquire good moral insight. He will receive praise forever." (Psalms 111:10)

Personally, I like seeking wisdom much more than I like seeking obedience. Wisdom is an intellectual exercise and can lead to being much admired. That appeals to me. Who doesn't want to be admired for being wise? Obedience, on the other hand, requires both inward attitude and outward action. While my parents and teachers appreciated my obedience when I was young, and my employers appreciated it later (when it happened!), the only person who truly *admires* my obedience is God. Yet I see that in many ways I crave the admiration of people far more than I do the admiration of God. It is a distressing thought.

I am almost overwhelmed by the thought that choice never stops. I will be choosing from now until I die, and every choice I make affects some other choice farther along my path. Obedience is and must be the polestar of all my choices.

****

Obedience to God is a consequence of our repentance. Obedience is not passive, it is active. Steve Castle once said, "Even Creation, in its proper order, by its nature, obeys the Creator; it is the broken creation that disobeys." We are obedient—we obey—when we *do* what God wants us to do. Action is also progressive. I am reminded of something Fr. Richard Somers said that has stuck with me over the decades. Fr. Somers described the ideal progression in our faith walk as involving:

- Knowing God's will
- Doing God's will
- Loving God's will
- Loving doing God's will

I think when we reach that last one we will finally understand something of what joyful obedience is all about.

****

Have you ever noticed we normally associate obedience with children? We think it's something we outgrow, something we no longer need once we have mastered self-control. In reality, obedience is a prerequisite for self-control. At the same time, we must be freed through Christ from ourselves and our sinful, selfish nature in order to be able to be obedient in the first place. This is a mystery I'm not entirely sure I understand yet, but increasingly I see the importance of it.

Obedience is the ugly duckling of virtues. Or perhaps it is the invisible virtue. You rarely see obedience even being mentioned when virtues are discussed. The classic seven virtues are: Prudence, Temperance, Justice, Fortitude, Faith, Hope, and Love. The fruits of the Spirit (Galatians 5:22) are: Love, Joy, Peace, Patience, Kindness, Goodness, Faithfulness, Gentleness, and Self-Control. No mention of obedience is made at all. Did you notice that? Obedience doesn't make a single list! However—not a single virtue or fruit of the Spirit is obtainable without obedience. So, much as a choice plant cannot produce its desired flower or fruit without adequate nutrition (think fertilizer), in the same way obedience may be considered the nutrition/fertilizer of our life of faith. We can grow without it, but we cannot flourish without it.

One day I was listening to a radio discussion about the beliefs of America's founding fathers. One comment about how self-control/restraint is a prerequisite for freedom caught my attention. The premise was, only people who are capable of self-control can be allowed to be free. People without self-control have no regard for others and must be restrained or constrained by increasingly severe rules/laws to the point where they are allowed no freedom at all. The final illustration given was a repeatedly lawless person who as a consequence of his actions ends up a prisoner with absolutely no freedom whatsoever. Thinking about that discussion, I was reminded of Brother Andrew, founder of Open Doors, whom I once heard say the reason dictators and other tyrants try so hard to suppress the Bible is because it is impossible to enslave a Bible-believing people.

****

CS Lewis, in his novel *That Hideous Strength* declares, "…obedience is an erotic necessity."[5] The context of the statement was advice being given to an unhappily married young woman. The first time I read it, I was appalled and not a little put off. But as I've come to understand obedience better, I think I understand what Lewis's point was.

If you've ever been deeply in love, you know that at the outset of the relationship your greatest joy comes from doing those things that delight your beloved. Without realizing it, when you do those things you are exercising a type of deep obedience. In this instance your obedience is to the desires of the other person, whether stated or understood. This sort of obedience creates a deep emotional intimacy, a sense of gratitude and appreciation. I think it is what Paul meant when he wrote, "In the same way husbands ought to love their wives as their own bodies. He who loves his wife loves himself. For no one has ever hated his own body but he feeds it and takes care of it, just as Christ also does the church." (Ephesians 5:28, 29)

****

Obedience is the filter through which we listen for the voice of God. Jesus said, "Anyone who doesn't obey Me doesn't love Me." (John 14:24a)

Many years ago I saw a billboard that said: "Listen today. Hear forever." I don't remember who sponsored the billboard, but I do remember the impact it had on me. The author of Hebrews (quoting Psalm 95) wrote, "Therefore, as the Holy Spirit says, "Oh, that today you would listen as He speaks! Do not harden your hearts as in the rebellion, in the day of testing in the wilderness." (Hebrews 3:7, 8)

Reading the Scriptures is an essential part of our filter. How can we obey if we do not know who or what it is we should be obeying? Where else do we find that but in God's Word? Reading the Scriptures with an expectation of hearing from God, of learning more about God is a form of joyful obedience, much the way one reads a love letter. Today I got the answer to a question I've long had about Jesus' genealogy while reading a footnote in Zechariah. Had I not been reading carefully, I would have missed it and the answer to my question.

It is important that we listen closely when we hear the Word of God, because it's so easy to become numb to the words. We tune them out ("I've heard that story a thousand times", "there's nothing new this preacher can teach me about this passage", etc.) and miss their meaning and import. I confess I am too often guilty of this. I need to remember hearing is a prerequisite to obeying. And refusing to hear means I risk losing the capacity to hear.

****

Corrie Ten Boom said, "Obedience is the proof of being a Christian. It is the gift of the Holy Spirit." Think about that for a few minutes. Now consider a few things Jesus said to that same effect:

> …If you continue to follow my teaching, you are really my disciples and you will know the truth, and the truth will set you free. (John 8:31, 32)

> Just as the Father has loved me, I have also loved you; remain in my love. If you obey my commandments, you will remain in my love, just as I have obeyed my Father's commandments and remain in His love. I have told you these things so that my joy may be in you, and your joy may be complete. My commandment is this—to love one another just as I have loved you. No one has greater love than this—that one lays down his life for his friends. You are my friends if you do what I command you. (John 15:9-14)

Strong words, aren't they? The apostle John understood this well when he wrote:

> But whoever obeys his word, truly in this person the love of God has been perfected. By this we know that we are in him. (1 John 2:5)

> For this is the love of God: that we keep his commandments. And his commandments do not weigh us down, because everyone who is fathered by God conquers the world. (1 John 5:3, 4)

Even the non-believing world is disappointed in disobedient Christians who don't live as they should. To have more and more of Jesus Christ in your heart is to be transformed into that new creation whose highest joy is in loving doing the will of God.

So far, we have looked at how obedience is defined and explored some related thoughts on those definitions. Both are largely intellectual exercises that lay an important foundation. To re-state what Fr. Richard Somers said, understanding what obedience is, is one thing. Cultivating a desire to obey God is another, and following through on that desire is quite another thing altogether. As part of that transition, here are a few things to consider:

- "When we learn to truly follow Jesus, we find that obedience to God comes from the inside out…what we do or don't do must come from who we are as followers of Jesus." (Kyle Idleman, *Not a Fan*)

- "If I don't obey Him, it means I don't trust Him with the possible consequences." (Charles Stanley)

- "When we don't fight against our sinful nature, sin wins. When we are disobedient, sin holds power over us. Sin never came out victorious in Jesus' life. When Jesus died on the cross, the sin nature in Him was completely defeated. In His humanness, Jesus could have chosen disobedience. But, in His humanness, He *chose* obedience, right over wrong, God's truth over fleshly desires. We can't obey God's laws on our own." (Karl Zorowski)

- "Disobedience is telling God, "You don't matter to me" or "You don't matter to me as much as I do." (Karl Zorowski)

Keep these in the back of your minds as we move forward in our exploration.

CHAPTER 3

Whom Do You Obey, and Why?

"Now obey the Lord and worship him with integrity and loyalty…If you have no desire to worship the Lord, choose today whom you will worship." (Joshua 24:14a, 15a)

It occurs to me that we are most often obedient to whomever or whatever is more powerful than we are. Perhaps it would be better stated that we are most often obedient to whomever or whatever we give power over us. (Doing a favor for a friend who asks is not obedience.) For some people that may be their own appetites. For others it may be their culture (peer pressure). Others give power—for better or worse—to family members: parents, spouse, and children. In the workplace we give power to employers as well as customers. Sometimes we give power appropriately and sometimes we don't.

As I was working on this section, I happened to be eating lunch in a favorite restaurant with my husband. Three young women were in the booth behind us, preparing for some sort of test or examination. One of them was reading their collective notes aloud to the other two. When she said, "the next topic is conflict resolution," I couldn't help but listen. Conflict resolution goes to the very heart of obedience. The young woman continued, "There are three things to consider: How much power do you have? How much do you value the relationship? How much time do you have to resolve the conflict?"

Hearing her was an "aha!" moment for me. To obey is to put yourself under the power of someone else. It is the ultimate form of humility. Obeying God means acknowledging that God is more powerful than you are. The more deeply we value relationships, the more often we choose to give the other persons power over us by acceding to their desires rather than our own. This is most often seen in a love relationship, where the delight of the beloved matters more to us than our own preferences. Also, the amount of time involved often determines how quickly we choose to obey. If your neighbor's house is on fire and someone tells you to call 911, you likely aren't going to challenge the directive. As Karl Zorowski has said, "In the kingdom, obedience is measured by what you do, not by what you say."

Bob Dylan stated a basic truth about obedience when he wrote the song, "Gotta Serve Somebody." I encourage you to take time to listen to this song in its entirety or at the very least look up the lyrics and read them slowly. Because when you remove all the trappings, all the excuses, all the rationalizations in your life, you either choose to obey God or you don't. It's that simple. And if you don't, whether you realize it or not, you're obeying the devil, who is hard at work keeping you disobedient. It was by the disobedience of rebellion that Lucifer, the most beautiful angel in heaven, became that adversarial creature we now call the devil.

Think about that for a moment. Any time you disobey God, the devil is giving you a standing ovation, cheering you on. If that's an image that makes your skin crawl, good!
If you disobey God long enough and persistently enough—even in the smallest things—eventually your actions will change you into something you're not going to like very much. As C.S. Lewis wrote in *Mere Christianity* (the "Forgiveness" essay), "Remember, we Christians think man lives forever. Therefore, what really matters is those little marks or twists on the central, inside part of the soul which are going to turn it, in the long run, into a heavenly or a hellish creature." In the same work (the "Charity" essay), he also wrote, "Good and evil both increase at compound

interest. That is why the little decisions you and I make every day are of such infinite importance."[6]

I am convinced we don't spend enough time thinking about the impact of our small acts of disobedience. I once attended a retreat where one of the speakers said the road to hell has steps so small we don't even notice when we've moved from one down to another. He said we can be halfway to the bottom (or more) before we look up and exclaim, "How did I get here?"

Serving God, on the other hand, is rarely a walk in the park. Jesus Christ obeyed God and it took Him through the agony of the crucifixion. Today's Christian culture by and large has made a huge deal out of Easter (and well it should, being the most momentous event in all human history), but it largely ignores the Passion. We've grown squeamish, which is odd considering the proliferation of graphic violence in movies and games. Church today is often all about positive, uplifting, feel-good experiences to attract as many people as possible. The danger is we're only giving half of the truth.

Years ago I experienced a profoundly moving, yet deeply painful, Good Friday service. Lying across the steps that led to the altar was a large wooden cross. Scattered around the cross were hammers and small bowls of nails. At one point during the service we were invited to come forward and actually hammer a nail into the cross while thinking about our own sins that held Christ there and for which He died. I accepted the invitation and all I'll say is it was one of the rawest experiences of my life. Some years later, I shared about this service with the church we were attending at the time. They decided to incorporate the cross and nails into their Good Friday service. I was surprised when afterwards, several church members complained loudly that they didn't want to do such a service ever again because it was so "unpleasant". Seriously?

There is no Resurrection without the Cross. There is no Easter joy without the suffering of the Passion. Vernon Small, a business associate of mine, observed during one of our small business roundtables, "Sometimes our deepest pain is the source of our greatest joy and our greatest joy is the source of our deepest pain."

To borrow from something Plato originally said about righteousness and apply it to obedience instead, obedience is often praised for the rewards it brings, but to see it in its true nature we must separate it from those rewards and strip it naked. Read the book of Acts sometime and you'll see the rewards of obedience don't always include happy outcomes from a human perspective. Hebrews Chapter 11 gets even more graphic about the fate of many who chose to obey God:

> But others were tortured, not accepting
> release, to obtain resurrection to a better life.
> And others experienced mocking and
> flogging, and even chains and imprisonment.
> They were stoned, sawed apart, murdered with
> the sword; they went about in sheepskins and
> goatskins; they were destitute, afflicted, ill-
> treated (the world was not worthy of them);
> they wandered in deserts and mountains and
> caves and openings in the earth. (Hebrews
> 11:35b-38)

It is so important to remember obedience is much larger than we can grasp. We don't know the true end of our own story, because we're limited in what we can see or understand. Lucifer lived face to face in constant contact with God, yet that wasn't enough for him, so disobedience entered the universe. Adam and Eve lived in a perfect paradise, in daily personal communion with God. It wasn't enough for them, so sin entered our world. We neither see God face to face, nor do we live in a perfect paradise. What chance do *we* stand of being successfully obedient to God when we are so often our own worst enemy? None without God's help. Without God's help we will surely be overwhelmed.

How can you even know if you're obeying God or not? One good way to begin is to learn as much Truth as possible. An excellent secular example of using truth to detect what is false is related by John F. MacArthur in his book *Reckless Faith: When the Church Loses Its Will to Discern*: "Federal agents don't learn to spot counterfeit money by studying the counterfeits. They study genuine bills until they master the look of the real thing. Then when they see the bogus money they recognize it."

Tim Challies did his own follow-up of McArthur's claim: "I can't count the number of times I have read quotes similar to that one, taken from John MacArthur's *Reckless Faith*…I have often wondered if this metaphor is accurate and whether agents truly study genuine currency first…It turns out that John MacArthur is correct. Training in identifying counterfeit currency begins with studying genuine money." Challies spent time at the Bank of Canada learning the process agents actually used and documented his experience on his website.[7]

We can find truth through reading the Scriptures and meditating on them. Listen closely to sound preaching and teaching, hopefully at the house of worship you attend regularly. Learn to look at life through God's eyes. Don't rely on your own understanding. Paul's admonition in Galatians still applies to us today:

> But I say, live by the Spirit and you will not carry out the desires of the flesh. For the flesh has desires that are opposed to the Spirit, and the Spirit has desires that are opposed to the flesh, for these are in opposition to each other,

> so that you cannot do what you want.
> (Galatians 5:16, 17)

This promise to the Israelites is also for those of us who have been grafted into the vine:

> The Lord will designate you for himself as a holy people just as he promised you, if you keep his commandments and walk in his ways. (Deuteronomy 28:9)

God Himself points out the simple truth that obedience is a choice:

> Then the Lord said to Cain, "Why are you angry, and why is your expression downcast? Is it not true that if you do what is right, you will be fine? But if you do not do what is right, sin is crouching at the door. It desires to dominate you, but you must suppress it." (Genesis 4:6, 7)

Although the website Snopes.com has debunked the truth of the story, the tale of the obstinate lighthouse provides an excellent illustration of how we spend too much time telling God to change course. In the story, of which there are many versions, a determined ship's captain keeps insisting another ship change course to avoid a collision. The other ship in turn demands he change course. In the final exchange, the other ship signals, "I am a lighthouse. *You* change course."

Obeying the wrong person brings destruction. Obeying the right Person brings life. Choosing to obey God—to do what is right—is a source of joy because your obedience gives glory to God. Choosing to refuse to obey God creates a point of weakness that gives sin an opportunity to attack and gain entry into our soul. To grasp the ever-present nature of sin's determined and almost patient waiting, picture the disease germs that are ever-present in our daily environment, waiting for an opportunity to attack the body at the first sign of weakness. We fight them off with proper nutrition, exercise, hygiene, and medicine when needed. So too we must fight sin with the proper nutrition (the Word of God), exercise (obedience to God), hygiene (keeping ourselves pure from the evil in the world), and medicine (when we succumb to sin, we use confession and repentance to bring healing).

CHAPTER 4

How Do You Obey?

As cited in the beginning of the Introduction, *The United Methodist Hymnal* "Service of Word and Table", prayer of "Confession and Pardon" contains a seemingly contradictory pair of words: "Free us for joyful obedience, through Jesus Christ our Lord."[20] Two important questions beg to be answered: How can obedience be a joyful thing? Is it even possible to actually *enjoy* obedience? Yes, I think it must be possible, that it *is* possible. In one of his sermons, Karl Zorowski said, "Joyful obedience means no longer reacting to an order or expectation; it is a way of living a life described (not proscribed) by God's laws."

I view obedience as a progression through four different levels, with joyful obedience being the goal towards which you grow. At its most basic level, obedience is blind; you do what you are told without giving any thought to the good or evil or even logic of it. Blind obedience follows orders, period. (Think of new military recruits undergoing basic training.) Usually no explanation is provided for the directions given, and there is no (or very little) emotional connection between the one giving the directions and the one following them.

Moving beyond blind obedience brings you to dutiful obedience—doing what you are told to do because it is the right thing to do or because it is your duty and obligation. In dutiful obedience, you usually receive some explanation of the reasons for following the directions. (Military personnel standing post on guard duty are a good example of this; they understand the reason for their duties.) However, like blind obedience, there is still little emotional connection between the one giving the directions and the one following them.

As you progress, you come to trusting obedience—doing what you are told because you believe the one directing you has your best interests at heart. Trusting obedience is similar to blind obedience in that there is often little explanation given for what you are told to do, but that matters less because there is a high level of emotional connection or intimacy between yourself and the one giving the directions. (Here I think of the relationship between a NASCAR driver and the spotter, a person positioned high above the track who directs the driver through often hazardous traffic the driver often cannot see.)

But there is yet another level of obedience to be reached, and it is the highest level of all: joyful obedience. Joyful obedience comes when you do what you are directed (or what is expected) because it is the right thing, done for the right reason, with the right attitude, and with the right expectation. In joyful obedience, you either understand the *why* behind the direction, or the *why* becomes irrelevant because of the trust and faith you have in the one you are obeying. In joyful obedience you share a high level of emotional intimacy with the one who directs you. Joyful obedience is not just a response; it is a gift you give to the one who calls you to obey. As the prayer of "Confession and Pardon" cited in the Introduction indicates, we must be *freed* for joyful obedience because we cannot get there on our own. It is something that only comes through a relationship with Jesus Christ when He is truly Lord in and of our life.

To me, these four levels of obedience correspond with the four steps I mentioned previously from Fr. Somers' homily on the progression of our faith walk:

- Knowing God's will→Blind obedience
- Doing God's will→Dutiful obedience
- Loving God's will→Trusting obedience
- Loving doing God's will→Joyful obedience

Or, as Adrian Rogers put it, "a slave obeys because he has to, an employee obeys because he needs to, and a loving son obeys because he wants to." Do you see the correlation?

- Slave→Blind obedience
- Employee→Dutiful obedience
- Loving son→Trusting obedience, Joyful obedience

We will explore all four levels of obedience in greater detail soon. But first, it's important to spend some time considering an essential prerequisite to any type of obedience: listening.

Obedience begins with listening. It is impossible to follow instructions if you haven't listened to them, and obedience is simply not possible without listening carefully. I've always thought of myself as a good listener, but just as I'm learning I know very little about obedience, I suspect I don't realize how little I actually listen in the normal course of my day.

Listening is a challenging exercise. It involves putting out of your mind all the other thoughts that try to intrude (and oh, my, how they do try to intrude!). Listening requires effort. It takes work to really listen to another person! In my own life I notice how often, when people begin telling me their problems, my normal inclination is to stop listening and think ahead to a solution. Reminding myself to "listen" disengages that process and lets me actually hear people and see each one as a precious creation of God.

Listening is one of the highest forms of courtesy. Listening and actually hearing can lead to obedience. One day a delightful older lady in her 80s telephoned our store to ask if we carried a particular product. I know her age because she began to tell me her life story early in the conversation. Initially my mind wandered and with the phone tucked between my neck and shoulder I started to work on other things while waiting for her to "wind down". Then I remembered to tell myself to *listen*. I stopped doing anything else and gave her my full attention; doing so allowed me to engage her in active conversation until she was ready to end the call. Similarly, God doesn't want me distracted when He wants to talk with me. He wants my full attention, knowing I cannot obey what I do not hear.

Listening implies understanding, being able to use and apply what we hear. We often think of a word's value as being its usefulness or applicability. We may continue to think about that later, but the strongest response comes at the initial hearing. Our willingness to let go of our desire to control our life reveals a certain trust. The more we trust, the deeper we go towards the joyful obedience that is so necessary, but so difficult.

What does this mean for joyful obedience? The baby in Elizabeth's womb leaped for joy at his first hearing of Mary's voice. The first time you heard the words "I love you" from that special someone, did your heart not leap for joy? Joy is an immediate response to hearing certain words, words that heal your heart. What is it we need to hear that we are not hearing from the Lord that keeps us from joyful obedience? Are we not hearing because we have chosen to make ourselves deaf inside a prison of our own making, the kingdom we have created in which we wear the only crown? Or are we just so busy in our own lives that God doesn't have a chance for us to even hear Him?

While listening is a prerequisite to any type of obedience, there is also a faith element that is perhaps the key ingredient to growing in obedience. I remember a time when I was frustrated by everything required before I could undergo a supposedly simple outpatient surgical procedure. I thought the pre-op cardiology clearance appointment a needless intrusion on my work schedule (not to mention the added expense!). My inner rebellion was finally quelled when I thought about it in terms of obedience. Perhaps what seemed unnecessary to me was not unnecessary to the surgeon. In the end I experienced active obedience and my attitude was better for it.

Let's look at the four levels of obedience in more detail. As I said before, I regard obedience as a progression. How we progress is a function both of the amount of information we are given and the degree of personal relationship we have with the one we obey. To express it in a chart:

	Degree of Personal Relationship	
Information	Low	High
High	Dutiful	Joyful
Low	Blind	Trusting

Blind obedience is at the lowest level, involving low amounts of information and a low degree of personal relationship. Dutiful obedience moves up the information scale, but it still involves a low degree of personal relationship. Trusting obedience moves to a higher level of relationship, but it often involves a significantly lower level of information than does dutiful obedience. Joyful obedience is the best of both, involving high levels of information (or understanding) and high levels of personal relationship.

Blind Obedience

Blind obedience is the most basic level of obedience. *Blind* is an appropriate illustration because with this type of obedience, you don't see either the reason for what you've been told to do or the outcome of it.

Blind obedience is an appropriate expectation of children who are too young to be able to understand that their actions have consequences. For example, young children are told, "Don't touch the stove". They usually aren't told why for several reasons. For one, they might not be able to understand. For another, explanations aren't necessary. The authority of the parent is sufficient in this instance. Blind obedience here is a good thing, because the consequence of disobeying could be a serious injury.

Blind obedience is also appropriate for adults in some types of work, especially work that is repetitive, such as is done on an assembly line. It isn't necessary to understand why the widget needs to be installed in a certain way, it is only necessary to do it that way. However, blind obedience can be a dangerous thing. Much harm has been done—especially in times of war—by people who did what they were told without question. "I was just following orders" rarely holds up well as a defense. James 4:17 gives the best answer to this (and the clearest definition of the sin of omission) I've ever read: "So whoever knows what is good to do and does not do it is guilty of sin."

Blind obedience can sometimes save your life. I know this from personal experience.

When I was a young teenager, I was invited to join my friend Diane's family on a picnic outing to a popular creek. I was excited to go because I always enjoyed spending time at this particular creek. It was wide, very shallow, and had a lovely sandy beach area. Imagine our surprise to discover that, due to recent rains, the lovely little creek had been transformed into a raging river. The water even covered the wooden footbridge that crossed the creek!

Not to be deterred, we picnicked on the bank. Diane and I were determined to walk across the handrail-less bridge, despite the three inches of water over it. We held on to each other for balance and were making excellent progress until the strong current sucking at our feet knocked me off balance. Letting go of her hand, I fell in and was immediately swept away.

Before I even had time to become afraid, I sensed a voice emphatically speak one word: *Relax*. I relaxed and cooperated with the water. Several hundred yards further, the creek made a sharp bend. As the water rushed around the bend, the force of it flung me against the bank, where I grabbed hold of some tree roots and pulled myself up to dry ground. Catching my breath, I picked my way along the bank back to my hosts. I did not fully appreciate the relief I saw on Diane's parents' faces until I was a much older adult.

In the Scriptures, God initially deals with people at the level of blind obedience if that's all they are capable of or if it's what the situation calls for (as when I fell into the flooded creek). Consider the conversion of Saul:

> Now on that day a great persecution began against the church in Jerusalem, and all except the apostles were forced to scatter throughout the regions of Judea and Samaria...But Saul was trying to destroy the church; entering one house after another, he dragged off both men and women and put them in prison...
> Meanwhile Saul, still breathing out threats to murder the Lord's disciples, went to the high priest and requested letters from him to the synagogues in Damascus so that if he found any who belonged to the Way, either men or women, he could bring them as prisoners to Jerusalem. As he was going along, approaching Damascus, suddenly a light from heaven flashed around him. He fell to the

> ground and heard a voice saying to him, "Saul, Saul, why are you persecuting me?" So he said, "Who are you, Lord?" He replied, "I am Jesus whom you are persecuting. But stand up and enter the city and you will be told what you must do."...So Saul got up from the ground, but although his eyes were open, he could see nothing." (Acts 8:1b, 3; 9:1-6, 8)

Now that's a case of truly blind obedience! Saul doesn't understand what happened or why. At this point he doesn't have any relationship with the unseen person he calls "Lord." However, a further reading of the passage shows Saul does as he's been told. After his sight is restored three days later, the murderer who was Saul becomes transformed into the apostle we know as Paul.

We see another instance of blind obedience in Mark 15:21: "The soldiers drafted a passer-by to carry his [Jesus'] cross, a man coming from the country, Simon of Cyrene, the father of Alexander and Rufus."

I think about Simon "coming from the country" when he was suddenly forced to carry the cross for Jesus. I imagine him to be an ordinary man on his way to the annual Passover festival, suddenly and for all eternity shoved onto the stage of history. It was blind obedience, to be sure—when the Roman soldiers grabbed him, did he even understand what was happening other than the awful reality that crucifixions were a regular part of their culture, and this was just one more in a long series of them? Simon likely was given no information. Certainly there was no personal relationship with the Roman soldiers—this was the forced obedience of someone under the iron fist of the Roman Empire. Despite this, I cannot help but wonder: as Simon looked at the horror of Jesus' wounds, perhaps something in him willingly rose up to help this helpless man. Did Simon even know who Jesus was? Had he heard of him? Perhaps after the Resurrection, in retrospect, Simon's experience may have been changed. So it often is with us. Often our obedience is forced from us by God's unyielding demands. Only later are we granted the insight that makes it joyful.

Ideally a relationship with God should move rapidly beyond the level of blind obedience. A careful reading of the Scriptures shows that God rarely expected purely blind obedience of anyone. Usually God gives sufficient information to explain why He asks what He does, even when the relationship is small or non-existent. Abram is an excellent example of this:

> Now the Lord said to Abram, "Go out from your country, your relatives, and your father's household to the land that I will show you. Then I will make you into a great nation, and I will bless you, and I will make your name great, in order that you might be a prime example of divine blessing." (Genesis 12:1-3)

When the Lord first spoke to Abram, Abram had no relationship with the Lord. Abram had no idea Who the Lord even was. I remember one television series on the Bible that depicted this specific scene. When Abram tells his father, "God spoke to me", his father asks, "which god?" Abram tries to explain to his father that it was none of the gods they knew and worshipped, it was a different God altogether. His father is confused and Abram admits he shares this confusion. Notice that God begins his message to Abram with the directive to "Go out", to leave everything that is familiar to him, without any known destination being provided.

While this appears to be a classic case of blind obedience, that isn't what God wants from Abram at all. What God is asking for here is faith. God is in essence asking Abram to leap from blind obedience to trusting obedience in one single step, to form a relationship with God that will be a prime example of divine blessing. When I read Scripture, this is the pattern I see most often between God and those who do not yet know Him.

Consider Moses, exiled from Egypt and the house of Pharaoh because of a murder he committed. Working as a shepherd for his father-in-law, Moses encounters God on the side of a mountain:

> Now Moses was shepherding the flock of Jethro his father-in-law, the priest of Midian, and he led the flock to the far side of the desert and came to the mountain of God, to Horeb. And the Angel of the Lord appeared to him in a flame of fire from within a bush. He looked—and the bush was ablaze with fire, but it was not being consumed! So Moses thought, "I will turn aside to see this amazing sight, why the bush does not burn up." And when the Lord saw that he had turned aside to look, God called to him from within the bush and said, "Moses, Moses!" And Moses said, "Here I am." And God said, "Do not come near here. Take your sandals off your feet, for the place on which you are standing is holy ground." He also said, "I am the God of your father, the God of Abraham, the God of Isaac, and the God of Jacob." Then Moses hid his face, because he was afraid to look at God. Then the Lord said, "I have surely seen the affliction of my people who are in Egypt. I have heard their cry because of their taskmasters, for I know their sorrows. I have come down to deliver them from the hand of

> the Egyptians and to bring them up from that land to a land that is both good and large, to a land flowing with milk and honey, to the territory of the Cannanites, Hittites, Amorites, Perizzites, Hivites, and Jebusites. And now, indeed, the cry of the Israelites has come to me, and I have also seen how severely the Egyptians oppress them. So now, go, and I will send you to Pharaoh to bring my people, the Israelites, out of Egypt." (Exodus 3:1-10)

Like Abram, what happens between Moses and God begins as blind obedience. The God Moses has only heard about, the God who seemingly has been absent for centuries and with whom Moses has no personal relationship, singles Moses out and directs him to be the deliverer of an entire nation—a nation held in bondage for hundreds of years. God gives no explanation of why Moses is to be the deliverer and Moses is understandably reluctant to accept the task. Moses presses God to show Himself trustworthy and God obliges, quickly moving Moses from blind obedience to trusting obedience (although I suspect a there may have been times during the forty years Moses spent leading the Israelites in the wilderness that he almost fell back to the level of dutiful obedience).

Given we have these and many other examples, it is unfortunate that so many Christians stop short in their pursuit of obedience, content to limit their faith journeys to what amounts to blind obedience. They know "the rules"—usually expressed as The Ten Commandments—but they can't explain to anyone why those rules should be obeyed other than "God said to do it this way." (Curiously, a detailed reading of The Ten Commandments reveals that God actually explains why the less obvious commandments are given! God, you see, is not a dictator.) Their relationship with God is not much of a relationship at all, being often limited to the single hour they spend in church on Sunday. Dust collects on their Bibles during the week, and God rarely hears from them in prayer, praise or—saddest of all—thanksgiving.

I think blind obedience that progresses no further is the result of weak faith. What miserable way it must be to live! God has so much more in store for us. One of the most startling bumper stickers I've ever seen proclaimed "Jesus is High Adventure." The first time I saw it, I couldn't wait to get one for myself. I was a new Christian and rapidly learning that everything about this new life was truly an adventure. (Apparently someone else didn't share my sentiment, because one night my car was vandalized by someone trying to tear the bumper sticker off it. I can only hope that what they read stayed with them until it eventually became truth).

My prayer is that if you're reading this at the level of blind obedience, you waste no time moving to the next level.

Dutiful Obedience

Dutiful obedience, based on adequate knowledge and information but lacking in relationship, is surely a dry, joyless thing. Often the motive behind dutiful obedience is simply to avoid discipline or punishment. At the level of dutiful obedience, you know and may even understand why you are following directions. However, you have no personal stake in the outcome; you don't see the big picture or the end results, and you have little or no personal relationship with the one giving you directions. Dutiful obedience, to me, is the drudgery class of obedience. It is, I think, the one that causes people to think Christianity is just not worth the effort. But, like everything else in the life of faith, it has its place.

For me, Hagar is an excellent example of dutiful obedience. (The entire story to which I'm referring is contained in Genesis Chapter 16.) Hagar was the Egyptian slave of Sarai,

Abram's wife. When the child promised by God did not come, Sarai took matters into her own hands. Following the accepted practices of her culture, Sarai pressured Abram into having a sexual relationship with Hagar to provide Sarai a child by what amounted to a secondary source. Abram agreed, and the Scripture notes, "Once Hagar realized she was pregnant, she despised Sarai." Hagar presumed on her status and tried to elevate herself by showing contempt for Sarai. Sarai responded by complaining bitterly to Abram, who told her, "Since your servant is under your authority, do to her whatever you think best." (In other words, Abram took the coward's way out.) What Sarai thought best was to act out her anger and treat Hagar harshly and, not surprisingly, Hagar ran away. I probably would have done the same thing. It's one reason many employees end up changing jobs.

The outcome is surprising, though:

> The Lord's angel found Hagar near a spring of water in the desert—the spring that is along the road to Shur. He said, "Hagar, servant of Sarai, where have you come from, and where are you going?" She replied, "I'm running away from my mistress Sarai." Then the Lord's angel said to her, "Return to your mistress and submit to her authority. I will greatly multiply your descendants," the Lord's angel added, "so that they will be too numerous to count." (Genesis 16:7-10)

I find this passage fascinating for several reasons. For one, Hagar was completely honest with the Lord. She answered the questions asked of her and without apology admitted she was running away from her mistress (in calling Sarai "mistress" she acknowledged what her true status was). I admire that she made no excuses, unlike so many other biblical characters. (However, can't you almost hear an implied, "If you'd had to put up with what I've had to, you'd run away, too!") The Lord responded by telling Hagar to exercise dutiful obedience: "return to your mistress and submit to her authority." The Lord also gave Hagar additional information about what will happen to her child and his descendants. There is an abundance of information, but there is no relationship between Hagar and the Lord's angel.

Being told to return and obey Sarai was probably the last thing Hagar wanted to hear. It was also probably not a surprise to her. Runaway slaves usually didn't get too far on foot in the desert. When Hagar returned to Sarai, I doubt Sarai gave her a warm reception. That Hagar didn't run away again is a source of amazement to me.

Like Hagar, many employees obey the rules and directions employers give them because it is what they must do to keep their jobs. (I've worked for harsh employers like Sarai, and it's not a pleasant experience.) I think many Christians all too often display a similar mentality in their faith lives and "follow the rules" simply to avoid hell or other divine punishment.

Ultimately it does always go well with us when we obey the Lord our God, but not necessarily the way we may think. We must be careful when we claim God's promises that we don't turn them into a type of incantation or magic charm.

Then there are those Christians who exercise dutiful obedience and "follow the rules" because they expect it is the way to eternal and temporal rewards—and who doesn't want the rewards? However, Jesus cautioned His disciples, "So you too, when you have done everything you were commanded to do, should say, 'We are slaves undeserving of special praise; we have only done what was our duty'." (Luke 17:10)

The scribes and Pharisees in Jesus' day were an excellent example of dutiful obedience. If dutiful obedience is knowing God's will and doing God's will without loving God or God's will, you can see why Jesus was so often exasperated by the Pharisees and their insistence on the letter of the law without any apparent understanding of the spirit of the law:

> On another Sabbath, Jesus entered the synagogue and was teaching. Now a man was there whose right hand was withered. The experts in the law and the Pharisees watched Jesus closely to see if he would heal on the Sabbath, so that they could find a reason to accuse him. But he knew their thoughts, and said to the man who had the withered hand, "Get up and stand here." So he rose and stood there. Then Jesus said to them, "I ask you, is it lawful to do good on the Sabbath or to do evil, to save a life or to destroy it?" After looking around at them all, he said to the man, "Stretch out your hand." The man did so, and his hand was restored. But they were filled with mindless rage and began debating with one another what they would do to Jesus.
> (Luke 6:6-11)

Do you see that last sentence? "They were filled with mindless rage." They could not rejoice in the healing because it violated the "rules" of the Sabbath.

Another time, Jesus was invited to a meal in the home of a Pharisee. When the Pharisee expressed astonishment that Jesus failed to do the usual ceremonial washing of his hands (this ceremonial washing had nothing to do with hygiene), Jesus used it as an opportunity to point out the hypocrisy of the Pharisees: "But woe to you Pharisees! You give a tenth of your mint, rue, and every herb, yet you neglect justice and love for God! But you should have done these things without neglecting the other." (Luke 11:42)

Notice that Jesus didn't have a problem with their dutifully giving what was expected. He did have a problem with the Pharisees and experts in the law being content with only excelling at dutiful obedience. One of Jesus' strongest indictments of the Pharisees and the experts in the law was when He exclaimed: "But woe to you experts in the law and you Pharisees, hypocrites! You keep locking people out of the kingdom of heaven! For you neither enter nor permit those trying to enter to go in." (Matthew 23:13)

In other words, the Pharisees didn't want a personal relationship with God and they weren't trying to help anyone else have a personal relationship with God. The Pharisees exercised dutiful obedience and nothing more. Because of that, they also wanted the people to do just their duty and nothing more. Sadly, when you consider how much like the Pharisees we can be in our own lives, is it any wonder so many Christians' lives are dry, dusty and joyless things where we do our duty and nothing more?

People who serve or have served in the military have an excellent grasp on what dutiful obedience means. Consider the New Testament story of the centurion whose servant was ill:

> After Jesus had finished teaching all this to the people, he entered Capernaum. A centurion there had a slave who was highly regarded, but who was sick and at the point of death. When the centurion heard about Jesus, he sent some Jewish elders to him, asking him to come and heal his slave. When they came to Jesus, they urged him earnestly, "He is worthy to have you do this for him, because he loves

our nation, and even built our synagogue." So Jesus went with them. When he was not far from the house, the centurion sent friends to say to him, "Lord, do not trouble yourself, for I am not worthy to have you come under my roof. That is why I did not presume to come to you. Instead, say the word, and my servant must be healed. For I too am a man set under authority, with soldiers under me. I say to this one, 'Go,' and he goes, and to another, 'Come,' and he comes, and to my slave, 'Do this,' and he does it." When Jesus heard this, he was amazed at him. He turned and said to the crowd that followed him, "I tell you, not even in Israel have I found such faith." So when those who had been sent returned to the house, they found the slave well. (Luke 7:1-10)

Although the centurion was exercising much more than dutiful obedience when he reached out to Jesus for help, he understood the principle so well that Jesus was amazed.

I remember reading a short story about a soldier given a sealed message to transport during wartime. He was given strict orders to not read the message. Despite this, his curiosity overcame him and he opened the message only to read: "The messenger is to be killed on sight." Terrified, the solider re-sealed the message and, pretending to be ill, asked a fellow soldier to deliver it in his place. His friend willingly obliged, leaving the first soldier to deal with the pangs of conscience he felt.

Much to the astonishment (and relief!) of the first soldier, the second soldier returned unharmed. It turned out the message was a code for the beginning of an important operation. The second soldier had been received with joy and even feasted by the commanding officer who received the message.

For me, the simple act of keeping my word is often a form of dutiful obedience. One time I had made a commitment to privately teach a woman on a Monday, which is normally my day off. It happened to be the Monday after the Daytona 500 NASCAR race, which is held on a Sunday afternoon. That year the race was rain-delayed to the point of having to be rescheduled for the following day—Monday. Knowing the Daytona 500 was to run at noon made me want to cancel my teaching commitment. However, I had made a promise to this woman and she was driving several hours from out of town for the class. It was my duty to keep my word to her and to show up with a good attitude. So I showed up with my best attitude. The class went well and there turned out to be a bonus. I discovered the woman was a sister in Christ, so we enjoyed some delightful conversation during our time together. I experienced joy in what I had expected to be nothing but dutiful obedience.

Oh, and there was a surprise bonus. Additional rain further delayed the start of the race until that night, so I didn't miss it after all! And while it was tempting to consider this a reward for obedience, I rejected that level of hubris and simply expressed gratitude for it.

God will accept dutiful obedience from us if that's all we are willing to give, but I think if we stop there God is deeply grieved. Again, God wants so much more for us!

Trusting Obedience

Like blind obedience, trusting obedience often involves your being given little explanation. Unlike blind obedience, however, trusting obedience involves a significant level of relationship with the one asking you to obey. You have reached the level of trusting obedience when you don't need to know *why* because you know and trust the character of the one giving you direction.

Trusting obedience is the act of a child who knows her parents love her. As I write this, there is a delightful commercial on television; one part of it depicts a father standing in a swimming pool with his arms outstretched to his little girl, who is standing hesitantly on the side of the pool. The man motions with his hands for her to jump and assures her he'll catch her. Finally she takes what is for her a huge leap and as her father catches her, she kisses him on the cheek. (That I can remember this scene but not the product for which the commercial was made means it failed utterly in its objective as a commercial...)

The chapter "Ears to Hear" in Ray Van der Laan's *Wandering with God in the Desert* talks about the dependence of the sheep upon the shepherd. Van der Laan points out that listening for the shepherd's voice is often a matter of life or death necessity for the sheep, so they know where to go and what to do. How curious that even sheep understand the need for trusting obedience, following only the voice of their specific shepherd and not that of a stranger. Jesus understood this when he said, "My sheep listen to my voice, and I know them, and they follow me." (John 10:27)

Karl Zorowski made an excellent point about this in one of his sermons on John 10:1-10: "Sometimes we follow the stranger's voice out of defiance; sometimes we have not learned to differentiate the Shepherd's voice from the stranger's. You either follow Jesus Christ or you don't. Knowing the Bible helps us know the Shepherd's voice."

When you read the book of Acts, you see incident after incident of trusting obedience. I am particularly struck by the story of Philip and the Ethiopian eunuch in Acts 8:26-40.

What an adventure followed Philip's obedience to the Lord's simple (but unexplained) instructions: "Get up and go south on the road that goes down from Jerusalem to Gaza." The passage notes that it was a desert road, so Philip would have had no expectation of anything unusual—other than it was the Lord sending him, which likely meant high adventure ahead. When you read the passage, realize that God took Philip down a *lonely* back road, something that often meant danger from robbers in those days. Yet when the Holy Spirit said "Go", Philip got up and went. He asked no questions—and took no time to pray about it first! He even *ran* to the stranger in the chariot when told to! Philip didn't go willingly on that road—he went obediently. He demonstrated trusting obedience and what a story he had to tell afterwards! Philip's obedience led him to an encounter with a powerful official of a foreign court and a seemingly unlikely potential convert. It also gave him the rather extraordinary experience of being literally carried away by the Spirit. The story reminds me of an unexpected encounter Rod and I had when we went to Bermuda for our fifth anniversary.

Prior to our trip, I looked up local churches and wrote the one closest to our hotel. I shared a little bit about us and inquired about their services, indicating that we planned to worship with them. Very quickly we received a letter in return in which their pastor referred to our "very exciting" letter. (When I mentioned this to our pastor and said I couldn't imagine what was exciting about it, he said "anytime people include worship as part of their vacation plans, from a pastoral viewpoint it's very exciting!") The Bermudian pastor asked us to plan on joining him and his wife for lunch the Monday after we worshipped together.

The shared worship time was delightful. Sunday evening the pastor called our hotel and asked if we had made plans for the early part of Monday morning before our scheduled lunch. He explained that Bermuda was a destination for many weddings and said couples came there from all over the world for their ceremonies. He was scheduled to perform a beach wedding for a German couple the next morning, but his two regular witnesses were unavailable. Would we be willing to perform that necessary function? We agreed, and what an adventure it was! I will never forget the experience of standing on that beach, watching the pastor in his formal Bermuda regalia of clerical collar, black Bermuda shorts and socks as he performed the ceremony. As I signed my name to the government record book, I prayed for the couple and thought of the importance of our witness. I was also reminded that if we had not been obedient to our commitment to worship, we would have missed this experience altogether.

When I meditate on the passage from Acts and Philip's experience with the Ethiopian official, I must ask myself: what have I missed out on by my disobedience, usually born out of fear, stubbornness or selfishness? Sometimes I think my disobedience comes from not knowing the outcome.

A Christian brother once shared the following experience during a small group session. He was driving home from an out of town trip when he felt the unmistakable voice of the Holy Spirit directing him to stop at a convenience store and purchase a gallon of milk. He initially dismissed it because it made no sense at all. He was almost three hours from home and had no need of milk. But he said he had no peace until he stopped and bought a gallon of milk. He then heard the Holy Spirit direct him to turn off on a specific road (one he didn't know) and deliver it to a specific house. Feeling like a fool, he made the turn and found the house. With not a little bit of trepidation, he walked to the front door and knocked, wondering how he would explain himself. When the door opened, the woman looked at the milk in his hand and before he could say anything, burst into tears and cried out, "Oh, thank you, Jesus!" She explained her child was sick and she had prayed for the needed milk she was not able to get. He told us it was the most amazing experience with God he had ever had.

Another Christian brother told us about his small men's group that met weekly for prayer. One of the members was terminally ill and no longer able to participate. At one of the meetings, another of the men said he had sensed the Holy Spirit directing them to pray over Jerry in absentia. So they laid a paper napkin on the table in front of them, anointed it with oil, laid hands on it as if it were Jerry, and prayed for healing. Then, still under the conviction of the Holy Spirit, they took it to Jerry and explained that he should eat the napkin. After they left, Jerry looked at the napkin for a long time. He thought the idea of eating it absurd, but at the same time he thought, *Why not? What do I have to lose?* So he got a large glass of buttermilk, and bit by bit he swallowed the entire napkin. Jerry went on to fully recover, something regarded as a miracle by those who knew him.

Karl Zorowski said something that reminded me of both of the above events: "If it comes from God, does it have to make any sense? The Messiah came to save the people from their sins, not from the Roman government, not from the marauding nations threatening them. We worship a living God, not a set of rigid rules."

God often issues His directives simply and without further explanation. He expects us to trust and obey. If I can remember that with Jesus lies the ultimate adventure, perhaps I can let go of my need to have control and simply obey.

Another excellent example of trusting obedience was Ananias:

> Now there was a disciple in Damascus named Ananias. The Lord said to him in a vision,

> "Ananias," and he replied, "Here I am, Lord."
> Then the Lord told him, "Get up and go to the
> street called 'Straight,' and at Judas' house
> look for a man from Tarsus named Saul. For
> he is praying, and he has seen in a vision a
> man named Ananias come in and place his
> hands on him so that he may see again." But
> Ananias replied, "Lord, I have heard from
> many people about this man, how much harm
> he has done to your saints in Jerusalem, and
> here he has authority from the chief priest to
> imprison all who call on your name." But the
> Lord said to him, "Go, because this man is my
> chosen instrument to carry my name before
> Gentiles and kings and the people of Israel.
> For I will show him how much he must suffer
> for the sake of my name." So Ananias
> departed and entered the house, placed his
> hands on Saul and said, "Brother Saul, the
> Lord Jesus, who appeared to you on the road
> as you came here, has sent me so that you may
> see again and be filled with the Holy Spirit."
> (Acts 9:10-17)

Now that is trusting obedience at its finest! Imagine God telling you to go lay hands on the worst dictator or the vilest offender you've ever heard of because God tells you He intends to use that person for the good of the kingdom. Isn't that similar to the situation when God initially called Jonah to go to Nineveh and preach? Unlike Ananias, though, Jonah said nothing but his action spoke volumes—immediately he ran away from God (or tried to; he didn't get too far). Ananias very likely wanted to run away as well, but instead he owned his fear and told God his deep concerns about this man Saul who hated the church so much.

I note with particular interest that God wasn't offended by Ananias' objection. Given Saul's history of violence against the followers of Jesus Christ—which extended to imprisonment and murder—Ananias had good reason to be concerned. However, he didn't ask for additional information because information wasn't what he needed. He did need reassurance and God gave it to him, along with some additional information. God is never offended by reasonable requests for reassurance or additional information when they are truly necessary to get us where we need to be in our obedience.

Sometimes trusting obedience involves God keeping you in a place or situation you'd rather not be. I remember a time, many years ago, when Rod and I were so frustrated with a church we attended that we wanted to leave. Before we did, though, we sought the counsel of a spiritual director we highly respected. I'll never forget his words. After agreeing with us that the issues with which we were concerned were, indeed, serious enough to warrant a church move, he then asked, "Has the Lord given you permission to leave?" We must have looked bewildered, because he added, "It may be that God wants you to remain where you are to be a witness or a provocation for change. It's important you understand what God wants of you in this situation." We ended up staying, and it proved to be an example of trusting obedience in my own life.

Recall that although Jesus certainly did not find the experience of the cross joyful, He went obediently, and His obedience was joyful. But even with joyful obedience, we may find ourselves obeying strictly on the basis of trust. Jesus trusted His Father: "Father, if you are willing, take this cup away from me. Yet not my will but yours be done." (Luke 22:42)

Reading Jesus' words, "not my will but yours", it occurs to me obedience doesn't require willingness, but it does require an act of the will.

I experienced this in a very personal way when I required surgery on my hand. After the surgery my hand hurt where the surgeon did his work. My post op instructions were simple: Don't try to use the hand until the surgeon cleared me to do so. When I obeyed and let the hand rest, the pain was less. If I tried to make my hand perform what it could not yet do, the pain increased. My flesh and nerves and muscles knew how to obey their Creator and do the work of healing. It was up to me to cooperate with that natural obedience or to impede it. I didn't have to be willing to do it, but I did have to exercise my will to be able to do it.

While preparing this section on trusting obedience, I came across a wonderful insight from *The Student Bible* (NIV Version) on Deuteronomy: "Deuteronomy focuses on motives: *why* people should obey laws. The preceding three books barely mentioned the love of God for his people, but Deuteronomy again and again refers to it (see 4:37,7:7-8,10:15,23:5). The author portrays God as a father with his children, as a mother who gives them life, as an eagle hovering over its young. In return, God asks for obedience based on love, not a sense of duty. At least 15 times in the book Moses tells the Israelites to love God and cling to him. God wants not just an outward conformity, but an obedience that comes from the heart."

> Jesus said to him, "Love the Lord your God with all your heart, with all your soul, and with all your mind." (Matthew 22:37, see also Deuteronomy 6:5)

Our David C. Cook Sunday School lesson one week addressed this same idea: "Just because something looks obedient on the outside doesn't mean it is being obedient on the inside…Inner and outer obedience to His decrees will keep us from falling apart personally and culturally—and will reflect His glory."

You have reached the level of trusting obedience in your relationship with God when you don't need to know *why* because you know the character of the One giving you direction. At this level you have the faith and the will to obey, and you can trust in God when you sense the Holy Spirit leading you. However, without a close personal relationship with Jesus Christ, this is as far as you can go in your relationship with God.

Joyful Obedience

Trusting Christians are interesting people to watch and listen to, but joyful Christians change the world. It was joy that caused the Christians to sing, even as they died, when Nero used them to light his garden parties. It was joy that kept Polycarp standing unbound against the stake as the fire was lit around him. It was joy that caused Paul and Silas to sing while chained in a Philippian dungeon. Until the Church today can get to the state of joyful obedience, she will never change the world. As Karl Zorowski has said, "It is joyful obedience that advances the cause of the Church, the work of the Church."

Joy is not the same as happiness. Happiness is a function of what happens to you. It is possible to create your own happiness, but you cannot create your own joy. There is a reason C.S. Lewis chose *Surprised by Joy* as the title for the book he wrote about his early life and spiritual journey. Joy surprises you because so often it comes when you least expect it. Joy is a gift from God. Joy is a fruit of the Holy Spirit.

In the story of Joseph and his brothers (Genesis 42-45) I see the progression of obedience. When the brothers come to Egypt to buy grain during the famine, they bow down before a Joseph they do not recognize, knowing only that this man holds absolute power over their lives. They are prepared to obey blindly, not knowing what is about to happen. When Joseph issues some strange orders and requires them to bring their brother Benjamin back with them, they obey dutifully—he is, after all, holding their brother Simeon captive and he is their only source of food in this ongoing famine. When, during their meal with Joseph, he tells them, "Come closer to me", although they are afraid and uncertain, there is a certain amount of trusting obedience shown. After all, this man has fed them and even though he just told them, "I am Joseph", surely he can't mean *that* Joseph, can he? Finally, Joseph tells them to go home and bring back their father Jacob and the rest of their families. Following that order can only have been met with joyful obedience. In Joseph they have met the only person who has the power to save them, and he has made known to them the full extent of his love for them.

What the Lord wants from us is trust and a willingness to obey. We cannot mature to the level of joyful obedience without our willingness to obey having fully matured.

The Apostle John understood that love and obedience are intertwined.

> Everyone who believes that Jesus is the Christ is fathered by God, and everyone who loves the father loves the child fathered by him. By this we know that we love the children of God: whenever we love God and obey his commandments. And his commandments do not weigh us down, because everyone who is fathered by God conquers the world. This is the conquering power that has conquered the

world: our faith. Now who is the person who has conquered the world except the one who believes that Jesus is the Son of God? Jesus Christ is the one who came by water and blood—not by the water only, but by the water and the blood. And the Spirit is the one who testifies, because the Spirit is the truth. (1 John 5:1-6)

Just as the Father has loved me, I have also loved you; remain in my love. If you obey my commandments, you will remain in my love, just as I have obeyed my Father's commandments and remain in his love. I have told you these things so that my joy may be in you, and your joy may be complete. My commandment is this—to love one another just as I have loved you. No one has greater love than this—that one lays down his life for his friends. You are my friends if you do what I command you. I no longer call you slaves, because the slave does not understand what his master is doing. But I have called you friends, because I have revealed to you everything I heard from my Father. You did not choose me, but I chose you and appointed you to go and bear fruit, fruit that remains, so that whatever you ask the Father in my name he will give you. This I command you—to love one another. (John 15:9-17)

In a sermon on these passages Paul Stallsworth pointed out Jesus said, "*If* you obey my commandments, you will remain in my love." He noted the *if* part is often missed. He also noted that Jesus' foremost commandment was "Love one another." I am struck by how we must be commanded to love those in the Body of Christ, which tells me love is not easy, nor is it a matter of natural compassion or emotion.

I also note that in 1 John 5, the word *keep* is synonymous with *obey*. There is a continual element to our expected obedience. It is not a once and done thing.

In another sermon Paul Stallsworth said, "Real faith moves towards joyful obedience. It is transformative."

Joyful obedience carries with it a sense of yearning: "O Lord, teach me how you want me to live! Then I will obey your commands. Make me wholeheartedly committed to you." (Psalms 86:11, 12)

Joyful obedience understands the highest good that comes from wanting to obey, because it is the way to obtain a deepening of intimacy with the One who asks for that obedience: "I have sung about your statutes in the house where you live. I remember your name during the night, O Lord, and I will keep your law. This has been my practice, for I observe your precepts." (Psalms 119:54-56)

Joyful obedience is only possible when we have an active, intimate relationship with Jesus Christ. Achieving intimacy in any relationship requires going far beyond just the rules that govern it.

Remember that most of the challenges Jesus faced from righteous people were about the rules. Jesus spent most of His time telling the rule-loving Jewish people that it wasn't about the rules so much as it was about the relationship behind the rules. The righteous Jews knew God's will and they did God's will, but they didn't love either one. Jesus was calling them to something higher and better than they could imagine and more often than not it infuriated them.

God called the Israelites out to be His special people to show the world what it meant to live in relationship with Him. They responded by wanting clarification. They wanted to know what the rules were—and nothing more than the rules—and they continued to "clarify" those rules until there was a rule and a sub-rule for everything. The chosen people preferred rules to relationship. It's so much easier to know what rules to follow and where the boundary markers are than to have to constantly deal with the tension of intimacy.

Adam and Eve had both. They had a deeply intimate relationship with God in a perfect environment. They also had one rule, because obedience is not really obedience without at least one boundary to observe, one test to pass, one opportunity to disobey. When they crossed the boundary and broke the one rule, they also destroyed the intimacy they enjoyed with God and each other. It took the work of Jesus Christ to restore to us that option.

Without the cross, we only have rules. But the work of Jesus Christ at Calvary restored our ability to enjoy intimacy with God our Creator. Don Francisco, in his wonderful song "Love is Not a Feeling," wrote, "Jesus didn't die for you because it was fun, He hung there for Love because it had to be done". Jesus suffered unspeakable pain for the joy that He knew would lay before us all.

The God who created the universe wanted a relationship with us, His creation. Can you wrap your mind around that incredible idea? God created mankind for intimacy with Himself. It was, and is, personal with God. And what was the response of the created to the Creator? When offered intimacy with God, people wanted rules. When God provided the rules, people responded by throwing over the rules with increasing frequency, further distancing themselves from God.

In *The Screwtape Letters*, C.S. Lewis wrote that to the devil our obedience is about His power, but to God our obedience is about His love.[8] God wants only the best for us—He wants servants who can become sons and He wanted it at the expense of His only Son.

Perfect obedience is the subject of numerous sermons. When I think of perfect obedience, I think of doing what God asks me to do, but doing it with enthusiasm and joy, in the right way, for the right reason, with no expectations of gain for myself. And that is impossible to do by or in my own strength. Only the Lord Jesus Christ, through the work of the Holy Spirit, can enable me to do even the smallest part of that. Again, joyful obedience is only possible through a personal relationship with Jesus Christ. We really have to be freed before we can experience it.

It is startling that Jesus' comments on obedience so often emphasized the familial aspect of obedience. (Indeed, obedience is a condition of a familial relationship with Jesus Christ.) But it is within our families that we deal with obedience on a daily basis, and it is within our families that we most often experience the loving, joyful aspect of obedience. Remarkably, Jesus said it is possible for us to actually be part of His family: "The one who belongs to God listens and responds to God's words." (John 8:47a) "For whoever does the will of my Father in heaven is my brother and sister and mother." (Matthew 12:50)

Jesus also talked about the obedience that exists only where there is love between friends:

> Just as the Father has loved me, I have also loved you; remain in my love. If you obey my commandments, you will remain in my love, just as I have obeyed my Father's commandments and remain in his love. I have

> told you these things so that my joy may be in you, and your joy may be complete. My commandment is this—to love one another just as I have loved you. No one has greater love than this—that one lays down his life for his friends. You are my friends if you do what I command you. (John 15:9-14)

This obedience of love is also implied in Galatians 6:2: "Carry one another's burdens, and in this way you will fulfill the law of Christ."

Haven't you noticed the closer the relationship you have with someone, the more joy you discover in obedience? Have you ever done something for someone you love simply because you knew how much delight would be received? That's what joyful obedience—passionate obedience, even—is all about: loving doing the will of God with grateful hearts because of the delight we know it gives the One to whom we owe so much. Gratitude is essential to experiencing joyful obedience. Experiencing the love of Jesus Christ is a necessity.

When we have grown to the point that we have maximum knowledge of and relationship with Jesus Christ and minimum interest in controlling our own lives or the lives of those around us, then and only then will we truly begin to know joyful obedience.

CHAPTER 5

The "D" Word—Discipline

In my opinion, Dr. Charles Stanley, Senior Pastor of First Baptist Church, Atlanta, Georgia is a master of summarizing essential spiritual truths. Not long after I started this study, I was riveted by his saying, "If I want to stay on track, obedience [to God] is the key." How true that is! Indeed, when I look back on the times when I got off track in my own life, I can correlate them to a specific moment of disobedience.

Dr. Stanley's reference to "staying on track" implies an athletic-type discipline. Athletes are often modern-day heroes, admired by many. Some athletes deserve that admiration and others do not. Few of us understand the level of discipline required to achieve athletic greatness. People who envy the skill of golfers like Phil Mickelson or Tiger Woods and wish they could play like those professionals rarely grasp the hours and hours of repetitive, tedious and often painful practice required. When swimmer Michael Phelps won an amazing eight Olympic gold medals, few in the wildly cheering crowd stopped to appreciate how many hours a day he spent in the pool to be able to reach his level of expertise. It is easy to forget that before the adulation of the crowds comes the discipline of the craft. In our increasingly "microwave" culture, where almost anything can be had instantly, discipline is becoming a lost art.

God challenged me to learn about discipline in an entirely new and personal way one New Year's Eve, as I was finishing my one-year study of the word obedience. I had dared to ask God what He would have me undertake for the next year. His reply was that it was time I learned about discipline (another of my least favorite words).

What God then inspired me to do was to sign up and begin training for the Multiple Sclerosis Society's 50-mile Challenge Walk. The annual event involves walking 50 miles over a three-day period as a fundraiser for the National MS Society. My beloved husband Rod has lived with MS almost half his life, and I was excited by the thought of being able to do something "for the cause". My excitement began to dim as the magnitude of the commitment I'd just made hit me. I almost panicked.

I am not, nor have I ever been, athletic. My talents have always been more cerebral than physical. I don't run well, I don't have the agility for gymnastics, I don't play ball-related sports well (the few times I have tried in the past subjected me to a great deal of ridicule). I lack the desire required to be an athlete. My entire personality leans more towards sprinting than it does marathons. I can put up with high levels of pain for a short period of time, but then I want it to be over with. It's one of the reasons I was very good in my academic studies. I could focus on very difficult coursework because I knew it would be over in a defined period of time. I could plan for it and even schedule my suffering, as it were.

Not surprisingly, I began training for the MS 50 with a cerebral exercise: I researched everything I could find on long-distance walking. I quickly learned that although I've been walking almost my whole life—it's the one activity I can do without much thought or effort—I knew absolutely nothing about long-distance walking. Therefore, the earliest part of my exercise in discipline was to learn from those who had gone before me.

Another part of the training involved the actual walking schedule. While the miles I was to walk became progressively longer, there were days on the schedule where the instructions specifically said, "Don't walk. This will allow the muscles to rest and repair." This idea of waiting didn't make a lot of sense to me at first, but as time went on it did.

Did you ever stop to think that waiting requires as much discipline (maybe even more) than doing? Until I trained for the MS 50, I don't think I had. I now believe obedience is also the discipline that keeps us waiting, as well as the action that tunes us into the ever deeper leading of the Holy Spirit.

As the number of training miles I walked increased, so did their difficulty. It became increasingly painful to walk and walk and walk and walk, hour after hour. Staying on the training schedule sometimes meant waking up at 5 am to be able to log the required training miles, which varied from 3 to 18 miles at a time. Because it was winter, sometimes the training involved walking in bitterly cold winds and even rain. Walking became work instead of a relaxing bit of exercise. Walking was no longer fun to do.

Why did I keep going when it would have been easier to quit? Because I honestly believed God had called me to complete this event to teach me something very important about discipline. On the long-walk days (when the distance I walked exceeded 10 miles), whenever the pain seemed almost unbearable, I would think about people who would gladly endure the pain I felt just to be able to walk again. I thought about the people who expressed their belief in what I was doing by making donations to the National MS Society as my sponsors. I found a new dimension to my prayer life as I thought about the endurance of the saints of God through the centuries. I thought about what Jesus suffered on the cross for me. Sometimes when I desperately needed to hear words of encouragement, I would call a friend and gain that encouragement from her as I walked.

By the date of the MS 50 Challenge Walk, I had logged 260 training miles in just over two months. I thought I was as prepared as I could possibly be, but I soon discovered I was mistaken. While attending the safety meeting the night before the event began, I learned a portion of the first day's 21.25 scheduled miles would involve walking over a high suspension bridge. I knew the route involved a bridge, but I had no idea the bridge was 2.7 miles long and 575 feet high!

When I came to the bridge, I stopped and took a deep breath. That 2.7 mile span seemed endless and almost dizzyingly high. I kept remembering what we had been told in the safety meeting, that once we started across the bridge, there were only two ways off it: to walk off or to be brought off in an ambulance. As I started over it, with traffic whizzing by me, I prayed and sang hymns, and before I knew it I was on the other side of the bridge, praising and thanking God for his faithfulness.

As the event progressed, the miles became increasingly hard; my muscles screamed in pain and several times I was tempted to quit. At one of my lowest points, with pain building from a fall earlier in the day and sheer exhaustion setting in, I sent my pastor a text message, telling him that I needed a prayer push in order to continue. Within seconds he replied, and soon I felt a new strength and energy.

On the third and final day I walked under the huge Finish banner and was greeted by a crowd—including Rod—all of them smiling and clapping. The joy I felt made the pain seem insignificant.

Notice that I did not experience the joy until after I experienced the discipline. I remembered the speaker I heard on the radio who said, "Obedience comes first, then the emotion." My joyful emotions after completing the MS 50 Challenge Walk did not come until after the obedience of actually doing the walk had reached its fullness.

Through this challenge I learned how necessary discipline is to completing any task that appears to exceed my abilities. I learned discipline sometimes involves action and it sometimes involves waiting. Discipline also involves humility—knowing what I do not know and learning from the lessons of those who have gone before me. I learned that discipline requires making room in our lives for something other than our normal routine. Henri Nouwen said that our busyness and preoccupation with ourselves leaves little room for the Holy Spirit Who "speaks when we are silent and who comes in whenever we have emptied ourselves."

The observance of Lent is an excellent time to practice discipline. Lent is often a struggle for many of us, and to truly worship during Lent is often a bigger struggle. To give up something for 40 days is not an easy thing to do. To take on something entirely new for 40 days can be even more challenging. Lent is a time in which we learn obedience can be both difficult and challenging, yet at the end of the process are wisdom and much grace. A desk sign I've long enjoyed proclaims, "The best way to get something done is to begin." I see that is how obedience works. We do not begin with joyful obedience. We begin with blind obedience and work our way up towards joyful obedience as we come to know Jesus Christ better and better and experience His love more and more fully and deeply.

During the year when I was studying obedience, I asked God what Lenten exercise He would have me undertake. The answer was, again, a single word: *Listen*. Practicing that one discipline caused me to stop and pause more often, which was good for me to do. It helped me listen rather than react to a harshly critical and anonymous email message from a person in my business network. It helped be guided by the wisdom of Proverbs 29:11 ("A fool lets out all his temper, but a wise person keeps it back") in developing my reply.

And by tempering my natural response, I inched forward in yet another small measure of obedience.

To be a person of prayer is another form of discipline. So many places in Scripture we're told, "Pray for one another." To pray requires a simple act of obedience, yet how often do we really do it? I know I have missed far too many opportunities for prayer in my own life. Because of that, I treasure opportunities like one I received when a woman came in the store to have a second look at a piece of fabric she'd seen the day before. She brought her mother along to get her opinion. While I spoke with the mother, I overheard the daughter on her telephone talking about a medical procedure. Her mother explained her 11-year old granddaughter was facing her second brain surgery for a tumor. My heart ached. Before they left, I asked the women if they would like a time of prayer for the child. They nodded and we held hands, forming a prayer circle. It was such a privilege to carry that need to the Lord!!

Perseverance, or endurance, is another essential aspect of discipline. One day I was listening to a Christian sports program; the topic was automobile racing. That particular weekend the longest races in both the Indy and NASCAR schedules were being held (500 miles and 600 miles, respectively). I was struck by the definition one speaker gave for endurance: "a long obedience in the same direction." His words reminded me of something I had seen the week before on the highway.

Runners from the State Highway Patrol were participating in the Special Olympics Torch Run. The lead group of runners ran with apparent ease, the leader proudly holding the torch high. A patrol car with flashing blue lights led the way. A second group of runners was close behind, also clearly athletic and running well; a police motorcycle followed them with lights flashing to keep them safe from approaching traffic. Then there was the last runner, at least a quarter mile behind the others. She was middle aged, overweight, perspiring heavily, and obviously struggling as she ran. Yet she ran with obvious endurance and determination. And close behind her was another patrol car with flashing blue lights, giving her the same protection as the others had received.

What a powerful illustration of the apostle Paul's message about running the race! Not everyone was running well, but they were all running their races with endurance—a long obedience in the same direction. And they all received the same protection as they ran. When I shared this story at church, someone shared another piece of the story. She said when she drove by she watched as the lead group of runners turned around and ran back to the slower woman, running with her for a time before they broke ahead again. What another powerful illustration of how we are called to encourage each other as we run our race!

Without discipline we will never understand humility, much less attain it. (Have you ever stopped to think of humility as a discipline?) Listening to a re-broadcast of Adrian Rogers' teaching on "Kingdom Authority" one day, I heard these words: "You will not be put *in* authority until you have learned to live *under* authority." A few moments later he added, "Submission is against human nature. But it does not mean acquiescence. The church is not the master of the State. The church is not the servant of the State. The church is the conscience of the State to preach God's truth." Wow! I had to take some time to chew on those words. Following—the thing we dislike doing—is a prerequisite for leading—the thing we prefer doing. Learning to obey God, to do the very thing against which we rebel with all our might, is critical to progressing in the leadership for which we long. We are still being formed and without discipline we cannot cooperate with God in the process.

Obedience implies there is something else I'd rather be doing if left to myself, which is why obedience requires a partnership with discipline. Within the Christian faith, discipline is not just something we do for our own benefit. Discipline is about making disciples. In one of his sermons, Steve Castle pointed out that to obey Jesus' instructions to make disciples requires not one, but three *I*'s: Instruction (church, Sunday School, Bible study), Imitation (1 Corinthians 4), and Immersion (sooner or later we get sent "out there" to make a difference).

I recall a story I heard about Arabian horses being trained in the desert. Trained with great patience and love to be devoted to the wishes of their master, their final test comes when they are penned high on a mountainside in the sweltering heat. Down at the bottom of the hill is a pool of cool water. The thirsty horses can smell the water. They long for the water and want it more than anything else. At last the gate is opened and the horses race towards the water. Then, just as they are about to reach it and satisfy their burning desire, the master blows the training whistle for them to come to him instead. Torn between their love of him and their strong desire for the water, the horses must decide which to choose. Those who turn around, at the very point of reaching their deepest desire, have passed their training. The master knows he can trust them. The horses who continue running towards the water have additional training to undergo.

I don't know about you, but on many levels I need additional training before the joy of obedience to my Master's call is more important to me than are the needs of my own life. In another sermon, Steve Castle said, "We're in a divine dance with the living God, breathing in and out the Holy Spirit. Jesus didn't say go and make friends; He said go and make disciples. And disciple-making is the work of the Holy Spirit."

Another illustration I find helpful is the concept of floating. Did you ever stop to think that a swimmer fights against the water to be able to go where the swimmer wants, whereas floating requires cooperating with the water, letting it take you where it will? And it actually takes effort to float successfully.

On the one hand it would seem impossible not to joyfully obey God if one fully knows Him. The more you know God, the more naturally you would obey—joyfully. Yet that was not the case with Lucifer and his followers. Not only did they refuse to obey—joyfully or otherwise—but they flatly rebelled. So there is another dimension to obedience, something necessary for it to be fully experienced, that I don't fully understand yet. Somehow it involves my free will and the need to discipline it properly.

> So then they said to him, "What must we do to accomplish the deeds God requires?" Jesus replied, "This is the deed God requires—to believe in the one whom he sent." (John 6:28, 29)

> [Jesus is speaking] Everyone who comes to me and listens to my words and puts them into practice—I will show you what he is like: He is like a man building a house, who dug down deep, and laid the foundation on bedrock. When a flood came, the river burst against that house but could not shake it because it had been well built. But the person who hears and does not put my words into practice is like a man who built a house on the ground without a foundation. When the river burst against that house, it collapsed immediately, and was utterly destroyed! (Luke 6:47-49)

It occurs to me how we often want the fruits of obedience without actually obeying. "Of course I will" becomes, in our own mind, the same as if we had actually done the thing.

> Understand this, my dear brothers and sisters! Let every person be quick to listen, slow to speak, slow to anger. For human anger does not accomplish God's righteousness. So put away all filth and evil excess and humbly welcome the message implanted within you, which is able to save your souls. But be sure you live out the message and do not merely listen to it and so deceive yourselves. (James 1:19-22)

We are so very good at fooling ourselves. We too often equate intention with actual obedience. We see that in the proliferation of New Year's resolutions each year. This is why there is a very real need for a serious Lenten observance. How long, really, is 40 days?

Even a successful Lenten discipline doesn't mean we've really learned something. Years ago I worked for a man who gave up cigarettes for Lent every year. And every year he picked them up again the Monday after Easter. Astonished, I would ask him why—once he had formed the healthy habit of not smoking—did he go back to his former practice? My question always made him laugh. He said it was his way of proving to himself that he could do it if he wanted to. He just didn't want to do it as a lifestyle change.

Obedience is the basis of any mental discipline. Growth in the Spirit comes as we deepen our level of obedience to the One who gave us the Spirit.

To recap some key points about discipline I learned from undertaking the MS 50 Challenge Walk:

- Discipline is about actions, not feelings. Feelings may bring desire, but actions bring results.

- Discipline sometimes is about doing good things you really don't want to do if left to yourself.

- Discipline sometimes is about not doing things you think make sense.

- Discipline keeps you from harm you might otherwise incur.

- Discipline means running (or walking) your own race and not worrying about how fast the others are moving.

- Discipline means walking by yourself at times with the confidence you are never really alone.

- Discipline follows the route signs and directions you've been given.

- Discipline knows there will be rough spots on the road—discouragement, weariness, and self-doubt—and mentally prepares to face them.

- Discipline knows that while yesterday's miles were important and necessary, you should be focused on the next mile.

CHAPTER 6

It Isn't Easy (Obstacles to Obedience)

Show me someone who says he enjoys being obedient and I'll show you someone who is either a fully perfected saint or someone who is not being honest either with himself or with others. Is obedience difficult? If you're new to it, not only is it difficult, it can seem almost impossible! It's like the rest of life: you don't get hungry until after you start the diet, and your nose doesn't itch until you're standing on stage ready to perform. In *Mere Christianity*, C.S. Lewis wrote, "No man knows how bad he is till he has tried very hard to be good."[10]

I have noticed the more I study obedience, the more aware I become that something in me—something both powerful and ugly—is rising up and crying out to rebel against the very idea of obedience. I understand in a new way what the apostle Paul meant he wrote:

> But I say, live by the Spirit and you will not
> carry out the desires of the flesh. For the flesh
> has desires that are opposed to the Spirit, and
> the Spirit has desires that are opposed to the
> flesh, for these are in opposition to each other,
> so that you cannot do what you want.
> Galatians 5:16, 17)

As already stated, "Creation, in its proper order, by its very nature obeys its Creator; it is only the broken creation that disobeys." So then, it is when I am broken that I am most in danger of disobedience and must be vigilantly on my guard.

I think another reason obedience doesn't come easily is because obedience can have a cost we are not willing to pay.

Literature is full of obedience tests that are difficult and full of obstacles. In my opinion, the best of these stories are found in the old fairy tales, the ones written and published before faith and prayer were edited out of them—especially those written by George MacDonald and Hans Christian Andersen. There is often a subtle message in these obedience tests, a message that echoes Jesus' warning to His followers: "…In the world you have trouble and suffering, but have courage—I have conquered the world." (John 16:33b).

One of my all-time favorite examples of obedience and suffering in literature occurs in George MacDonald's remarkable book *The Princess and Curdie*. In this story, the princess' fairy grandmother Irene has summoned the miner's son Curdie to give him a valuable gift, a gift that will help him save both her son the king and her beloved young granddaughter. Curdie, who knows Irene well, has every reason to trust both her wisdom and her power. Irene tells him the trial she has for him requires only trust and obedience, but she adds it will hurt him terribly although much good will come to him from it. Then she instructs him to walk over to the fire of roses on her hearth and thrust his hands fully into it. The imagery MacDonald's words convey at this point are powerful:

> Curdie dared not stop to think. It was much too terrible to think about. He rushed to the fire, and thrust both of his hands right into the middle of the heap of flaming roses, and his arms halfway up to the elbows. And it did hurt! But he did not draw them back. He held the pain as if it were a thing that would kill him if he let it go—as indeed it would have done. He was in terrible fear lest it should conquer him.

> But when it had risen to the pitch that he
> thought he could bear it no longer, it began to
> fall again, and went on growing less and less
> until by contrast with its former severity it had
> become rather pleasant. At last it ceased
> altogether, and Curdie thought his hands must
> be burned to cinders if not ashes, for he did
> not feel them at all.

I have taken much encouragement from this passage during critical times of suffering in my life. It reminds me to lean into the pain, trusting that the One who directs me is aware of my suffering, indeed is suffering with me, and plans great good to be the end result.

Oh, I should add that the end result of Curdie's trial is revealed when he withdraws his hands. To him they look the same. However, he learns the trial has gifted him with the ability to tell a person's true character simply by touching their hands.

Real life, like literature, is also full of obedience tests, many of which often go unrecognized at the time. There's an excellent example portrayed in the contemporary movie, "Courageous." In the movie, a prayerful man named Javier is desperately seeking work to support his family. Through a series of providential events, he obtains a job in a local factory and works very hard. His diligence is noticed. One day Javier is called to the office of the factory owner and offered a promotion to supervisor. The owner tells the excited Javier he must first work a probationary night shift in the shipping and receiving department before being promoted to the new position. Javier eagerly agrees. Then the factory owner explains that he wants Javier to log in only twelve of thirteen expected shipments, saying he had something else planned for the thirteenth shipment. When Javier looks confused, the factory owner suggests he go home and think about it and give him an answer the next morning. He also stresses how important he considers teamwork to be.

Javier is an anguished man as he struggles between his conscience and his desire to succeed. The next morning as Javier enters the office, the factory owner smiles warmly and asks him if he's made a decision. Javier nods and explains he cannot do what's been asked of him. The factory owner stops smiling and demands to know why. Javier has a simple answer: "It would be lying; it would shame my family and my God." The factory owner asks if Javier has considered the implications of this answer for his regular job. Javier nods, his head down. He doesn't see the slight smile that passes between the factory owner and his manager as the owner exclaims, "Congratulations!" Javier looks up to see an outstretched hand and a smiling face as the factory owner explains he'd almost given up finding an honest employee. At last Javier understands he's faced—and passed—a serious test of character. Honesty is a child of obedience.

Control and our desire for it are at the very core of the issue of obedience and why it is anything but easy. Eve was tempted by the serpent's promise, "You will be as God." In other words, you will be in control of everything in your life. Who doesn't want that? To be truly obedient, on the other hand, is to surrender control completely. On those days when I struggle desperately with obedience in my innermost being, I realize in how many ways I am truly a daughter of Eve, wanting to be as God in my own little kingdom. And even though my sins of omission far outweigh my sins of commission, they are no less sin.

Proverbs 8:33 adds to this thought: "Listen to my instruction so that you may be wise, and do not neglect it." Neglect is a form of disobedience. It's a passive, seemingly benign form of disobedience to be sure, but a deadly one no less.

It Isn't Easy (Obstacles to Obedience)

One Sunday Steve Castle made some interesting points about how we often throw ourselves out as an obstacle to what God asks of us; we become too comfortable in who we are to be available (read that obedient) to God. We sit on our faith rather than acting on our faith. Steve reminded us that God will call us, irritate us, pester us, but God will never force us. All this reminds me that obedience will always be left as our choice: "This is the end of the matter, having heard everything: Fear God and keep his commandments, for this is the whole duty of man." (Ecclesiastes 12:13, 14)

It sounds like such a simple arrangement: obey God and He takes care of all the rest. To know God—truly know God—is by definition to obey God, for there is nothing in the character of God that should cause us to not want to obey. So, then, when we refuse to obey, it shows the extent to which we yet do not know God.

It is important to realize God has a purpose in mind for each of us, and our obedience is necessary for Him to be able to give us all the good He intends. "Consider this: When I spoke to your ancestors after I brought them out of Egypt, I did not merely give them commands about burnt offerings and sacrifices. I also explicitly commanded them: 'Obey me. If you do, I will be your God and you will be my people. Live exactly the way I tell you and things will go well with you'." (Jeremiah 7:21-23)

While we can find many ways to fool ourselves, it's no good trying to fool God by sounding noble in our prayers as our defense. As Proverbs 21:2 says, "All of a person's ways seem right in his own opinion, but the Lord evaluates the motivations." In other words, we can justify everything we do but God looks at our motives.

The One who created us knows us better than we know ourselves. C.S. Lewis, in his autobiography *Surprised by Joy*, once wrote to the effect that he thought a serious sin committed from an act of desperation may, to God, be considered less serious than a trivial sin committed from a malicious intent to wound.[10]

Every act of obedience on our part molds us more into who God created us to be. Every act of disobedience warps us more and more out of shape. God warned the Israelites that some of His promises were conditional, that He would not do some things if they made certain choices: "But in the same way every faithful promise the Lord your God made to you has been realized, it is just as certain, if you disobey, that the Lord will bring on you every judgment until he destroys you from this good land which the Lord your God gave you." (Joshua 23:15)

How is it that obedience is the simplest—and at the same time the most difficult—thing to do? There is an insightful study note in *The NET Bible* when Moses first appears before Pharaoh in obedience to God's command: "When the people of God attempt to devote their full service and allegiance to God, they encounter opposition from the world. Rather than finding instant blessing and peace, they find conflict." Things got worse before they got better, just as they later did for Joseph.

The writer of Psalm 119 recognized the need for determination: "The enemies who chase me are numerous. Yet I do not turn aside from your rules." (Psalms 119:157, 158) Although the psalmist is speaking of external enemies, we know too well that our enemies are often internal—our own desires and ambition are enemies as real as any that exist outside us.

Let's look at some specific obstacles to obedience we must overcome:

Fear

Fear is a paralyzing emotion. Deep fear can literally shut down your ability to move or even speak. Stop for a minute and think about the last time you were really, *really* afraid. Yes, it's not a pleasant exercise, but there's a point to it.

What thoughts went through your mind? Were you able to pray? Could you admit your fear, or were you too proud or too ashamed to do that, even to God? Is it any wonder that fear is probably the number one obstacle to obedience? To stare down your fear and do what God asks in spite of it is probably the hardest thing imaginable. There are several excellent examples in the Bible of people who did just that. Too often we read their stories and rush past the reality of the fear they must have felt. Let's stop and taste that fear with two of them: Moses and Esther.

Take some time to read the book of Exodus (well, at least the first 15 chapters of it). It's important to get an understanding of Moses' background to fully grasp the depth of his fear when it hits him. Moses was raised from infancy in the house of Pharaoh, where he was presumed to be the son of Pharaoh's daughter. His was a noble, privileged life. His future looked assured. Then suddenly he found himself an outcast, on the run for his life under a death sentence from his own (supposed) grandfather.

Decades later, Moses has made a new life for himself in the desert, working as a shepherd for his father-in-law. Perhaps he missed his former life of ease; perhaps he didn't. It's doubtful he thought much about it by then.

God gets Moses' attention through the burning bush, telling him, "So now, go, and I will send you to Pharaoh to bring my people, the Israelites, out of Egypt." (Exodus 3:10). How terrifying must that have been? Moses *knew* what waited for him back in Egypt. He had a wife and two sons and a good life where he was. Who was this God, anyway? And yet—and yet—Moses obeyed God.

Now read the book of Esther. I think we tend to overly romanticize much of this story, forgetting that King Xerxes was actually a brutal, cruel and ruthless man (historical sources portray him as dangerously impulsive). The book of Esther records that the king loved Esther and chose her as his wife, but we are not told whether Esther loved him. (There is a slightly longer Greek version of Esther that portrays Esther as deeply unhappy about her situation.) It was in such an environment that Mordecai asked Esther to go to the king and plead for the life of her people, the Jews.

Esther was afraid. I imagine she was absolutely terrified. She knew the unpredictable nature of her husband meant she was as likely to be brutally killed as she was to be kissed. But despite her fear, Esther used all the resources at her disposal as she walked the path of obedience: first she asked for a three day fast on her behalf; then she used the status of her rank to face the king, arrayed in her royal robes. Her obedience glorified God and God responded by honoring her obedience. She and her people were spared and the Jews still celebrate that deliverance each year in the feast of Purim.

In a sermon titled "Rough Seas of Transition", Steve Castle focused on Mark 4:35-41:

> On that day, when evening came, Jesus said to his disciples, "Let us go across to the other side of the lake." So after leaving the crowd, they took him along, just as he was, in the boat, and other boats were with him. Now a great windstorm developed and the waves were breaking into the boat, so that the boat was nearly swamped. But he was in the stern,

> sleeping on a cushion. They woke him up and said to him, "Teacher, don't you care that we are about to die?" So he got up and rebuked the wind, and said to the sea, "Be quiet! Calm down!" Then the wind stopped, and it was dead calm. And he said to them, "Why are you cowardly? Do you still not have faith?" They were overwhelmed by fear and said to one another, "Who then is this? Even the wind and sea obey him!"

Steve pointed out this is a teaching opportunity for the church today; our storms are storms of doubt and confusion, often prompted by fear. But if we are following Jesus, why are we so often afraid? Do we, like the disciples back then, still have no faith?

In another sermon titled, "Onward Christian Soldiers" (based on Matthew 12:46-50 and 28:16-20), Steve Castle said, "Jesus' primary claim on us is to radical obedience. We must muster the courage to do whatever He asks of us." Now that's an interesting concept: radical obedience! But then, especially in our culture, the very thought of obeying God is a radical thing, isn't it? The culture says do what you want, do what makes you happy, that's all that matters. But God, as always, knows better, doesn't He?

Steve went on to say that discipleship is about keeping and honoring commitments. (In other words, it's about obedience.) He said what people see out of us can make a total difference in their lives. He asked if we wanted to be spiritual sequoias or spiritual bonsai trees. He also asked what we were afraid would happen if we began to actually make disciples of all nations. Changing that up just a bit, I wonder what would happen if we actually began to radically obey the demands of Jesus Christ.

Telling people God wants them to follow their dreams is easier than telling them, "take up your cross and follow Jesus". But as Rachel Jankovic said on Dr. *James Dobson's Family Talk* radio program, "Obedience to God in your whole life puts your dreams up for grabs." We are often so deeply afraid of what God will ask us to do that we are paralyzed, and that shows how little we understand the character and the love of God.

When people reject our efforts to share the love of Jesus Christ and the hope of the Gospel, they don't reject us—they reject God and His word because they want an easier way to God and to heaven. So why do we give up when people reject the Gospel? Often it's because we're afraid. But God doesn't bend to fit into our fears. God wants to take us to that place beyond fear, where "There is no fear in love, but perfect love drives out fear" (1 John 4:18a).

Confusion

People often claim they are confused when they are looking for an excuse to avoid obedience. I once heard a radio talk show counselor scold a caller who complained, "I'm so confused I don't know what to do." The counselor shot back, "No, you're not confused. You know exactly what you need to do. You just don't want to do it and you're using the word 'confusion' as an excuse."

Sometimes, though, we truly are confused. Life can deal us some terrible blows and some of them knock us so off our emotional balance we can't think or see clearly. I remember one such time in my own life. My grandfather had died and when I heard the news, I felt nothing. I truly didn't care. I was at the time still dealing with the effects of some inappropriate behavior from years before. I wanted to care about his passing, but I honestly couldn't find a way to get there. On my way into evening church services, I walked past

It Isn't Easy (Obstacles to Obedience)

a group of people I knew well. When they asked me how I was doing, before I knew it I'd replied, "Not very good. My grandfather just died and I don't care." They nodded and one of them gently said, "Sometimes it happens that way." I was profoundly relieved to be accepted where I was at that moment rather than criticized for such an un-Christian attitude. Later during the service I asked one of them to pray with me at the altar rail. I'll never forget his prayer: "Lord, sometimes life becomes so confusing that confusion itself becomes the feeling. Please heal and clarify the confusion in Patti's life so she can see and hear You clearly again." What a magnificent prayer that was!

Confusion can result from a lack of a standard. One day, while listening to a re-broadcast of J. Vernon McGee on the radio, I was intrigued by his illustration: "Evil has a mystery to it and that's why it appeals to people. If I tell you I'm holding a stick straight as a ruler, you would all draw it the same because you know what straight looks like. But if I tell you I'm holding a crooked stick, there would be a million different drawings, because there are a million different ways the stick could be crooked." I think obedience is drawing the straight stick. There is no confusion with Jesus Christ or with obedience to Him when we know who He is.

Confusion can be caused by an inability to correctly process information. During a Sunday Homecoming service, Steve Castle said: "The church is suffering from missional Alzheimer's. We don't know who we are, Whose we are, or why we are." It was a good illustration of confusion becoming an impediment to obedience.

Sometimes we are confused because God doesn't work the way we think He should. In Isaiah 55:8, 9, God said, "Indeed, my plans are not like your plans, and my deeds are not like your deeds, for just as the sky is higher than the earth, so my deeds are superior to your deeds and my plans are superior to your plans." I'll never forget the time a woman at church joyfully announced, "I've decided God no longer owes me an explanation of how He runs the universe. It's been quite freeing, actually."

We don't have to understand God to obey Him. And we don't have to be confused because we don't understand. When we don't understand and are confused, we must exercise trusting obedience to be able to struggle through our confusion. Note how struggle doesn't accompany blind or dutiful obedience, and confusion doesn't accompany trusting or joyful obedience. "O Lord, teach me how you want me to live! Then I will obey your commands. Make me wholeheartedly committed to you." (Psalms 86:11, 12)

Many people in the Bible experienced confusion, with varying degrees of impediment to obedience. Max Lucado, in *Cast of Characters*, wrote, "Joseph didn't let his confusion disrupt his obedience." I love that example! Can you imagine a more confused young person than Joseph was in Genesis chapters 37 and 39-45? One minute he's his father's pampered favorite. The next minute his jealous brothers throw him into a pit, intending to kill him. Before Joseph knows what's happening, he's pulled out of the pit and sold as a slave, first to a travelling caravan and then to Potiphar, the captain of Pharaoh's guard. Then, in the prime of his youth and full of raging hormones and unfulfilled passions, he's thrown into a daily struggle with the openly expressed desires of Potiphar's neglected wife. Falsely charged with attempted rape, he's thrown into prison. Suddenly he's pulled out of prison and brought before Pharaoh to interpret a dream. Almost before he knows it he's the number two official in Egypt and (unrecognized by them) facing the brothers whose jealous hatred sold him into slavery in the first place. Joseph had so many opportunities to be disrupted in his obedience to God, and yet each time he held fast to what was true and right.

Confusion may be an obstacle to obedience, but it is never an excuse for it.

> Therefore, keep the terms of this covenant and obey them so that you may be successful in everything you do. (Deuteronomy 29:29)

> Walk as children of the light…trying to learn what is pleasing to the Lord. Do not participate in the unfruitful deeds of darkness, but rather expose them. For this reason do not be foolish, but be wise by understanding what the will of the Lord is. (Ephesians 5:8b, 10, 17)

> …remember all the commandments of the Lord, and obey them; so that you do not follow after your own heart and your own eyes that lead you to unfaithfulness. (Numbers 15:39b)

Doubt

When asked to name a biblical character who struggled with doubt, most people would likely name Thomas.

> Now Thomas (called Didymus), one of the twelve, was not with them when Jesus came. The other disciples told him, "We have seen the Lord!" But he replied, "Unless I see the wounds from the nails in his hands, and put my finger into the wounds from his side, I will never believe it!" (John 20:24, 25)

But we tend to forget Thomas wasn't the only disciple who had trouble believing the resurrection of Jesus:

While they were saying these things, Jesus himself stood among them and said to them, "Peace be with you." But they were startled and terrified, thinking they saw a ghost. Then he said to them, "Why are you so frightened, and why do doubts arise in your hearts? Look at my hands and my feet; it's me! Touch me and see; a ghost does not have flesh and bones like you see I have." When he had said this, he showed them his hands and his feet. (Luke 24:36-40)

Then he appeared to the eleven themselves, while they were eating, and he rebuked them for their unbelief and hardness of heart, because they did not believe those who had seen him resurrected. He said to them, "Go into all the world and preach the gospel to every creature." (Mark 16:14, 15)

So the eleven disciples went to Galilee to the mountain Jesus had designated. When they saw him, they worshipped him, but some doubted. Then Jesus came up and said to them, "All authority in heaven and on earth has been given to me. Therefore go and make disciples of all nations, baptizing them in the name of the Father and the Son and the Holy Spirit, teaching them to obey everything I have commanded you. And remember, I am with you always, to the end of the age. (Matthew 28:16-20)

How often have you heard someone say—or perhaps said it yourself—"if only I had lived when Jesus did and seen Him myself, it would have been easy to believe in Him and obey Him?" The implication is that "those days" were somehow different from "our days". The people who knew Jesus best—and not just Thomas—, who lived and worked beside Him for three years, *doubted* Him.

Steve Castle asked a very pointed question in his sermon, "Trusting God on the Bumpy Roads": "Why is obedience so hard?" He gave a fascinating three-part answer:

1. The Jesus I expect may not be the Jesus I get.
2. We may think it's over when in reality it's the beginning of something more than we could ever hope for.
3. We cling to the bad news when the good news is standing right beside us.

All three of these have been true in my life. How about yours? Doubt is a common thread to all three. Jesus shattered every preconceived notion the Jews had about what the Messiah would be like. They had two choices: change their preconceived notion or refuse to believe (i.e., doubt). Beginning with the arrest of Jesus, the disciples saw their dreams of deliverance from Rome's cruel authority smashed. Peter's doubts made him think everything was over, so he denied even knowing Jesus in an effort to save himself. When the risen Jesus Christ encountered two of the disciples on the road to Emmaus, their despair and doubt made them blind to Who He even was until the breaking of the bread.

Never underestimate the power of doubt to derail your faith journey. Let's look at a truly heartbreaking Old Testament example of the disaster doubt can create: Saul.

Doubt caused Saul to lose his right to the throne barely a week after Samuel anointed him to be the first king of Israel. 1 Samuel Chapter 10 begins with Samuel giving Saul a specific list of signs he would soon encounter. Verse 6 ends with Samuel telling Saul, "You will be changed into a different person." Then in the next two verses Samuel continues by telling Saul, "When these signs have taken place, do whatever your hand finds to do, for God will be with you. You will go down to Gilgal before me. I am about to come down to you to offer burnt offerings and to make peace offerings. You should wait for seven days, until I come to you and tell you what to do." Verse 9 says, "As Saul turned to leave Samuel, God changed his thinking. All these signs happened on that very day."

Saul had been given every assurance of the promise made to him. God had even changed his thinking (or as the Hebrew puts it, "God turned for him another heart")—in effect, caused his conversion. One week later, doubt had stolen it and God revoked Saul's right to rule as a consequence. Let's read together what happened:

> For the battle with Israel the Philistines had amassed three thousand chariots, six thousand horsemen, and an army as numerous as the sand on the seashore. They went up and camped at Michmash, east of Beth Aven. The men of Israel realized they had a problem because their army was hard pressed. So the army hid in caves, thickets, cliffs, strongholds, and cisterns. Some of the Hebrews crossed over the Jordan River to the land of Gad and Gilead. But Saul stayed at Gilgal; the entire army that was with him was terrified. He waited for seven days, the time period indicated by Samuel. But Samuel did not come to Gilgal, and the army began to abandon Saul. (1 Samuel 13:5-8)

Can you feel the doubt as it creeps into Saul's heart and mind? *Who is this prophet named Samuel, anyway? Am I really expected to just wait for him to show up and offer sacrifices? Is he even coming? Am I really king over this people? How can I lead my army when they're already running away because they're so afraid?* Doubt, driven by fear and confusion, pushes Saul to take matters into his own hands and he presumptuously offers the sacrifices in Samuel's place. What happens next is heartbreaking in the reality it describes:

> When he had finished offering the burnt offering, Samuel appeared on the scene. Saul went out to meet him and to greet him. But Samuel said, "What have you done?" Saul replied, "When I saw that the army had started to abandon me and that you didn't come at the appointed time and that the Philistines had assembled at Michmash, I thought, 'Now the Philistines will come down on me at Gilgal and I have not sought the Lord's favor.' So I was compelled to offer the burnt offering." Then Samuel said to Saul, "You have made a foolish choice! You have not obeyed the commandment that the Lord your God gave you. Had you done that, the Lord would have established your kingdom over Israel forever. But now your kingdom will not continue." (1 Samuel 13:10-14)

At the very moment Saul's doubt caused him to give up on God's promise and disobey, what was promised appears. Samuel's pointed question, "What have you done?" is the same question God asked Eve back in Genesis 3:13. Samuel's attempt to excuse and justify himself didn't work, just as Eve's attempt to excuse and justify herself didn't work (and just as our attempts to excuse and justify ourselves will never work with God). Samuel called Saul to accountability with two simple truths: "You have made a foolish choice" and, "You have not obeyed the commandment that the Lord your God gave you."

Steve Castle gave a sermon on "Why I Believe in God", taken from John 1:1-18, in which he said: "There are times we doubt God, even His very existence. Obedience gets us past that. Obedience is the narrow footpath through the desert places. We have to have faith to be able to doubt." Saul believed God, but his belief didn't relieve him of his doubts when the time of testing came. Saul's doubts proved to be, for him, an insurmountable obstacle to obedience.

So what do we do with our doubts? I think the apostle Thomas showed us the best thing to do: own them, make a reasonable request and give God room to work. Look back at when Thomas said, "Unless I see the wounds from the nails in his hands, and put my finger into the wounds from his side, I will never believe it!" (John 20:25) Some people are very critical of Thomas for his doubt and what they see as a challenge to God. I see it differently. I think Thomas' doubt, although very real and potentially debilitating, was an honest emotion that he wasn't afraid to admit. But notice he didn't just say, "I will never believe it!" Thomas gave God room to work by also admitting what he needed to be able to believe. Thomas *wanted* to believe. Others had seen Jesus and he needed to see Jesus, too—see Him *and* touch Him. It was not an unreasonable request. Jesus never had problems with reasonable requests and He didn't have problems with honest doubt. Thomas doubted and Jesus answered that doubt with Himself.

My friend Jeff told me of a time when he struggled with doubt and how God answered him as generously and completely as He had Thomas. His story is so compelling that I asked him to allow me to share it in his own words. It is long, but it is also unforgettable:

I had reached a point where I was struggling with doubt, wondering if God was truly there. It is important you understand that for years prior to this, God had been very real to me. I would often pray during the day and, just as often, God would put it on my heart to pray for someone or make a change in my life. These promptings were very specific, very clear, and not ideas I would have come up with on my own.

Things changed for me when I felt the Holy Spirit prompting me to pray for the father of a good friend of mine; I'll call the father "Jack". Jack had been diagnosed with cancer and treatment wasn't going well. The prompting was very clear: I was to meet with Jack, ask him if he believed God would heal him, and then pray out loud with him, placing my hands on him for his healing in the name of Jesus Christ. This was far beyond any task God had ever asked of me. I seriously doubted God would use me to bring direct healing to someone I barely knew. I could only imagine the scene: I would approach Jack and the moment would be very awkward; I would clumsily say the prayer, nothing would happen, and then I would forever doubt God had really spoken to me.

So I refused to approach Jack at all, despite continued promptings and a sense of increasing urgency almost nagging on my heart to pray with him. Within a few weeks Jack died and the promptings to pray for him stopped. What was worse, I no longer heard God speak to me at all and no longer had any promptings to make changes in my life or to pray for others. I felt alone, and when I prayed it felt like God was no longer even there! I began to convince myself I had never really had any communication with God and that it was all stuff I had made up in my head. I needed to stop wasting my time praying for God to speak to me again.

The problem was I couldn't stop! The emptiness in my heart and my longing for God began to interfere with both my personal life and my ability to focus at work. Often by lunch time, I couldn't stand it any longer and would kneel down in a private place and just cry, tears dripping onto my uniform as I prayed God would once again speak to me and let me feel His presence

My world was falling apart, both personally and professionally. I got passed over for a major promotion, which was a huge embarrassment professionally. My original transfer orders were cancelled and I was given different orders to a less desirable location, only to discover my wife and I could neither sell nor refinance our home, as we were nearly $200K upside down from the market crash that occurred right after we bought it. It seemed like nothing was going right and God was punishing me.

In the middle of all this I got sent to a conference out of state. I was going alone and would be driving in my car for almost six hours each way. I hoped the long quiet ride would give me time to pray, listen for, and

It Isn't Easy (Obstacles to Obedience)

(hopefully) hear God again. On the other hand, it would be a grueling and frustrating drive if I continued to hear nothing.

On the drive down, I left the radio off so I could listen for God without distraction, but I heard nothing except the hum of the tires. Frustrated and angry, I wondered why God had abandoned me and why everything in my life was falling apart. When the conference was over, I headed home using a familiar route. Not wanting to be disappointed by still not hearing from God, I decided to turn the radio on and listen to one of my favorite Christian radio stations, the one I had enjoyed when I used to live in Jacksonville. (Now, this was before I had satellite radio in my car and the only problem with this particular station and the route I was driving is, it doesn't take very long once you get outside the city limits before you lose signal reception.) When I lost the signal I turned the radio off to get rid of the static noise. And then I got mad!

I spoke to God out loud as if He was in the car with me. I asked Him to prove He was real, to give me a sign as He had done with Gideon in the Book of Judges. I boldly told God if He was real, then when I turned the radio back on, I would hear the exact same song that had been playing when I lost the signal. I turned on the radio and that very song was playing! After my initial shock, I rationalized, this really proves nothing. I was in an area where the radio signal frequently comes and goes. This isn't a sign from God, I told myself, this is just the coincidence of when I turned the radio on. By the time I finished that thought the radio went static again. I turned it off and then I thought: When the music came back on, wasn't the song at the *exact point* where I had first lost the signal?

I continued driving, and after several minutes I turned the radio back on. Nothing. I wondered, Should I ask God a second time and put Him to the test? Gideon was so bold to ask God twice. I had driven much farther by now and turned the radio on again. Nothing, just static. I was definitely out of range of that radio station at this point. I reasoned if I asked God and heard that same song again at this distance, there would be no question it was a sign from God. I felt convicted that what happened next would forever end my doubt. But what if it didn't? I turned the radio on again to confirm that nothing except static came out of the speakers. It had been more than an hour since the last time I heard music playing on the radio. Facing my fears, I asked God again to play the same song as before when I turned the radio back on. Pulling over to the side of the road with my heart racing in my chest, I turned the radio on to hear…*the same song*, playing just as clearly as before. I listened for a few seconds, turned it off, and cried.

There was such relief in knowing God had answered my cry for Him to reveal himself. I started driving again, but soon feelings of anger and frustration started bubbling up inside me again. Finally I yelled out, "What do You want from me"? For the first and only time in my life, I heard God speak to me as clearly if He was sitting beside me. It was not the typical experience where you hear a voice in your head or a feeling on your heart. In a very firm tone and loud enough to not let there be any doubt, God stated, "Obey Me". God didn't need to say any more. I understood now. As the events since my refusal to pray for Jack's healing flashed through my mind, I realized that in order to hear from God, I had to be willing to obey God.

And with that, Jeff's problem with doubt was finally resolved.

If honest doubt is the only thing standing between you and your ability to obey God, rest assured God is bigger than your doubt. God won't violate your trust, but God will exceed your expectations. So, if you have doubt, trust the Lord Almighty "to see if I will not open for you the windows of heaven and pour out for you a blessing until there is no room for it all." (Malachi 3:10b)

Shame

Shame is an unpopular word in today's culture, but I think there is still a place for shame. There are over 100 references to shame in the Bible. Shame can come one of two ways: shame can be imposed on a person from the outside, or shame can be internalized. Both can be taken to a point of abuse, and that's when shame is a very bad thing. But both can be instruments that lead to repentance, and that's a very good thing.

Shame that leads to repentance is a great catalyst for obedience. It's the false shame lingering on after repentance, locking you up inside yourself, that is the obstacle to obedience. We need to understand there is a difference. But God is bigger than both types of shame.

Peter is an excellent example of both types of shame. Not only did he deny knowing Jesus after having publicly sworn, "Even if I must die with you, I will never deny you" (Matthew 26:35), Peter did it three times, the third time with curses. At the very moment his curses began, Peter heard a rooster crow. The gospel of Matthew records: "Then Peter remembered what Jesus had said: 'Before the rooster crows, you will deny me three times.' And he went outside and wept bitterly." (Matthew 26:75) Bitter weeping is a sign of a heart broken by recognized shame.

Jesus was keenly aware of the ongoing shame in Peter's heart and soul, as these verses indicate:

> But go, tell his disciples, even Peter, that [Jesus] is going ahead of you into Galilee. You will see him there, just as he told you." (Mark 16:7)

> Then when they had finished breakfast, Jesus said to Simon Peter, "Simon, son of John, do you love me more than these do?" He replied, "Yes, Lord, you know I love you." Jesus told him, "Feed my lambs." Jesus said a second time, "Simon, son of John, do you love me?" He replied, "Yes, Lord, you know I love you." Jesus told him, "Shepherd my sheep." Jesus said a third time, "Simon, son of John, do you love me?" Peter was distressed that Jesus asked him a third time, "Do you love me?" and said, "Lord, you know everything. You know that I love you." Jesus replied, "Feed my sheep."...After he said this, Jesus told Peter, "Follow me." (John 21:15-17, 19b)

How kind of our Lord to make sure the angel specifically included Peter in the invitation! Nothing short of that would likely have freed him from the shame of his denial. Peter the Rock had crumbled like sandstone when the time of testing came. Imagine how Peter must have felt when he heard, "Yes, Peter, the angel specifically said you were to be there, too."

The first Don Francisco song I ever heard was the extraordinary, "He's Alive", that tells the story from Peter's point of view. Do look it up and listen to it sometime. The lyrics are powerful, but the way Don sings them conveys everything Peter surely felt: despair at having been a self-serving coward when he'd sworn to be loyal to the point of death; frustration that his three years with Jesus had been wasted time; doubt that he'd ever have any part in a resurrected Jesus' kingdom. And then, "Jesus stood before me, with His arms held open wide, and I fell down on my knees and just clung to Him and cried."

Once Jesus got Peter past his shame, the next thing He did was call him to obedience: "Follow Me." And Peter did—for the rest of his life.

Are you struggling with shame being imposed on you from outside for something beyond your control? You're not alone. In the Bible, Judges Chapter 10 tells the story of Jepthah, the illegitimate son of his father's union with a prostitute. Luke Chapters 5 and 17 tell of lepers—utter outcasts in their culture—who sought and received healing from Jesus. Luke Chapter 19 tells the story of Zaccheus, the despised tax collector. John Chapter 4 tells of the Samaritan woman who had been married and divorced five times and was living with a sixth man who wouldn't even bother to marry her. Her shame was so deep she went to the well in the heat of the day to draw water, rather than having to face the other women at the normal time for that task. But her encounter with Jesus healed her soul and sent her running to the townspeople to share the wonderful news she'd just received.

Jesus can break the chains of shame other people have placed on you, too. Luke Chapter 8 tells of Jesus' healing a demoniac who lived among the tombs. The man begged to go with Jesus, and I think a part of that desire was to not have to face the shame that he would likely meet from his family and friends. But Jesus told him, "Return to your home, and declare what God has done for you. So he went away, proclaiming throughout the whole town what Jesus had done for him." (Luke 8:39) Do you see that? Jesus broke not only the chains that held him at the tombs, but also the chains that might have been placed on him going forward. Jesus freed him from shame for the purpose of obedience, and the man obeyed.

Are you struggling with shame over things you've done or failed to do in your life? Again, you're not alone. In 2 Samuel Chapter 11 we read the awful story where King David turned to murder to try to hide his adultery with another man's wife. Acts Chapters 8 and 9 tells how Saul (who would become the Apostle Paul) persecuted Christians to jail and even death before he met Jesus Christ on the road to Damascus.

Paul later wrote in 2 Timothy 1:3a, "I am thankful to God, whom I have served with a clear conscience…" Paul was able to say he served God with a clear conscience despite the irreparable damage he'd done to so many people's lives. Paul understood and embraced the full depth of forgiveness Jesus Christ offered him. Jesus Christ offers that same forgiveness and cleansing to each one of us.

If ongoing shame over something you've done or left undone is an obstacle to obedience, ask yourself these questions:

Have I fully repented of this? Have I fully confessed it to God and accepted His forgiveness? Have I made amends—as far as possible without doing further damage—to those my actions have harmed? Have I placed appropriate boundaries in my life to help ensure it never happens again? If you can answer "Yes" to all these questions, you are dealing with false shame and need to let it go and get on with doing whatever God is calling you to do. (If there's a "No" in your answers, then you need to get with God quickly and deal with it!) Once Jesus Christ has removed our shame and freed us to follow Him, we must not let *anyone* put those shackles back on us.

My own life has not been lived in a straight line. But I give deepest thanks that the God Who writes straight with crooked lines has made my life a forward progression. Many years ago, my spiritual director loaned me his copy of J. Neville Ward's *Five for Sorrow, Ten for Joy: Consideration for the Rosary*. Ward was a United Methodist minister, and his book explored the Catholic prayer known as the Rosary. In one part of the book, Ward wrote, "No one turns to God and stays with Him forever. The process of turning has to be repeated again and again. Through these repeated returns, confessions, forgiveness, recommitments, renewals of trust, one grows in the knowledge of God."

Proverbs 24:16a says, "Although a righteous person may fall seven times, he gets up again." Don't let shame over your forgiven past keep you down—or disobedient!

Pride

C.S. Lewis called pride "The Greatest Sin". He said, "it was through Pride that the devil became the devil: Pride leads to every other vice: it is the complete anti-God state of mind."[11] The 19th century minister and author George McDonald said, "The one principle of Hell is—'I am my own'."

Dante, fourteenth century author of The Divine Comedy said, "Pride is love of self, perverted to hatred and contempt for one's neighbor." Karl Zorowski pointed out this is the antithesis of Christian perfection!

The eighteenth century theologian Jonathan Edwards said, "Nothing sets a man out of the devil's reach so much as humility." Humility is the virtue that is opposite the vice.

Now, it's important to be clear what is meant here by pride. The pride I'm talking about should be spelled prIde, because it is all about the *I*. C.S. Lewis wrote, "Pride is not taking a healthy satisfaction in doing a task to the best of your ability or knowing you pleased someone you wanted to please. Pride the vice is competitive; it doesn't just want, it wants more of whatever than anyone else has. Pride is about having, especially about having power."[12]

PrIde is a huge obstacle to obedience, because prIde by its very nature cannot obey anyone or anything else. Athletes—even those with immense natural talent—often fall prey to prIde. Every sport has rules to ensure fair competition. The Apostle Paul often referred to athletics in his letter to the early Church: "Also if anyone competes as an athlete, he will not be crowned as the winner unless he competes according to the rules." (2 Timothy 2:5)

Because prIde will not follow rules, an athlete consumed with prIde will try to find ways around the rules. The cyclist Lance Armstrong had great talent and was much acclaimed for his victories, but apparently he had too much prIde to rely on his talent alone. The scandal about his doping cost him his titles, his reputation, and his livelihood.

In the Bible, 2 Kings Chapter 5 tells the story of Naaman, a man who is full of prIde.

Now Naaman, the commander of the army of the king of Syria, was esteemed and respected by his master, for through him the Lord had given Syria military victories. But the great warrior had a skin disease. Raiding parties went out from Syria and took captive from the land of Israel a young girl, who became a servant to Naaman's wife. She told her mistress, "If only my master were in the presence of the prophet who is in Samaria! Then he would cure him of his skin disease."

Naaman went and told his master what the girl from the land of Israel had said. The king of Syria said, "Go! I will send a letter to the king of Israel." So he went, taking with him ten units of silver, ten thousand shekels of gold, and ten suits of clothes. He brought the letter to the king of Israel. It said, "This is a letter of introduction for my servant Naaman, whom I have sent to be cured of his skin disease." When the king of Israel read the letter, he tore his clothes and said, 'Am I God? Can I kill or restore life? Why does he ask me to cure a man of his skin disease? Certainly you must see that he is looking for an excuse to fight me."

When Elisha the prophet heard that the king had torn his clothes, he sent this message to the king, "Why did you tear your clothes? Send him to me so he may know there is a prophet in Israel." So Naaman came with his horses and chariots and stood in the doorway of Elisha's house. Elisha sent out a messenger who told him, "Go and wash seven times in the Jordan; your skin will be restored and you will be healed." Naaman went away angry. He said: "Look, I thought for sure he would come out, stand there, invoke the name of the Lord his God, wave his hand over the area, and cure the skin disease. The rivers of Damascus, the Abana and Pharpar, are better than any of the waters of Israel. Could I not wash in them and be healed?" So he turned and went away angry. His servants approached and said to him, "O master, if the prophet had told you to do some difficult task, you would have been willing to do it. It seems you would be happy that he simply said, "Wash and you will be healed." So he went down and dipped in the Jordan seven times, as the prophet had instructed. His skin became as smooth as a young child's and he was healed. (2 Kings 5:1-14)

I am fascinated by the story of Naaman and its continuing truth today. Naaman desperately wants healing, but he wants it his way. He wants his healing to be commensurate with his stature and position in life. He wants Elisha to greet him personally, to put on a show for him. Naaman wants the dramatic and he gets none of it.

What Naaman gets instead is simplicity. Elisha is not only unimpressed by Naaman's display of power (note the horses and chariots), he completely ignores it—and Naaman. Elisha simply speaks for God, and Naaman misses the connection at first. Elisha understood that obedience isn't about the show or the flashy thing. Naaman doesn't see that obedience to the simple is the harder task. Fortunately for him, his servants know how to appeal to his reason and when he obeys the simplicity of the directions given to him, he is healed. Like Naaman, we must hear and obey. Only then can we be healed. Between the hearing, and the obeying, however, we must get rid of our prIde.

> The one who despises instruction will pay the penalty, but whoever esteems instruction will be rewarded.
> Proverbs 13:13
>
> The one who deals wisely in a matter will find success, and blessed is the one who trusts in the Lord.
> Proverbs 16:20

Naaman lost his prIde, discovered obedience and received healing as a result. Where in your life is prIde an obstacle to obedience and healing?

Blame

Blame seems to be ingrained in our DNA. What is the default excuse of even a very young child? "I didn't do it, _____ did it." "_____ made me do it." "It's not my fault. It's _____'s fault."

The first sin, recorded in Genesis 3, was disobedience. The second sin was blaming it on someone else:

> The man said, "The woman whom you gave me, she gave me some fruit from the tree and I ate it." So the Lord God said to the woman, "What is this you have done?" And the woman replied, "The serpent tricked me, and I ate." (Genesis 3:12, 13)

Notice neither Adam nor Eve ever said, "I'm sorry." I have often wondered what would have happened if they had said, "Father, I/we disobeyed You. I/we have no excuse. Please forgive me/us." Would there have still been consequences? I believe so. Sin always has consequences. But the outcome might have been more like that experienced by the Prodigal

Son, who took full responsibility for his disobedience. (If you think the prodigal escaped consequences, you haven't read the full story. The father did not restore the inheritance the son squandered, and under the culture of that day he was going to live as a dependent of his older brother for the rest of his life.)

In my own family of origin, blame was the normal response to everything. Sadly, I had a brother who—to his dying day—blamed the failures of his life on our parents. If it had not been for the work of the Holy Spirit in my life, that would likely have been my story as well. Thankfully God transformed that part of me (or at least a large part of me).

I still remember the first time I exercised the new attitude. It was at work, where blame was also the normal response to everything. Procrastination on my part had put a project for which I was responsible behind schedule. When asked what happened, I looked my director in the eye and said, "It's my fault. I dropped the ball. I'll have it finished by the end of the week." I cannot describe the freedom I felt! And then I watched in astonishment as my director picked up his phone, called the vice president who had begun the inquiry, and laid the blame for the delay on another department's failure to give us key information we needed in a timely manner.

Progress in obedience is simply not possible as long as we indulge in the "blame game".

Selfishness

Selfishness just seems to come naturally to most of us. We've been dealing with it since we were children. How often did our parents have to remind us to share?

I remember my father asking for a bite of my candy bar when I was very young. I didn't want to share it, but I also didn't dare tell him that, so I offered it to him. To my horror, his "bite" took almost half the bar. "There, doesn't it taste better when you share?" he asked cheerfully. I don't think I said anything, but inside I was yelling, "No, it doesn't, because you took too much!"

That was an example of selfishness at its worst. Selfishness quite simply is not wanting to share what you have. Sometimes selfishness is prompted by a fear of not having enough left for yourself. Sometimes selfishness is the result of greed or pride, where you think you win by having the most of whatever it is you won't share.

Jesus encountered a person who struggled with selfishness in Matthew 19:16-22:

> Now a man came up to him and said, "Teacher, what good thing must I do to gain eternal life?" He said to him, "Why do you ask me about what is good? There is only one who is good. But if you want to enter into life, keep the commandments." "Which ones?" he asked. Jesus replied, "Do not murder, do not commit adultery, do not steal, do not give false witness, honor your father and mother and love your neighbor as yourself." The young man said to him, "I have kept all these things. What do I still lack?" Jesus said to him, "If you wish to be perfect, go sell your possessions and give the money to the poor, and you will have treasure in heaven. Then come, follow me." But when the young man heard this he went away sorrowful, for he was very rich.

Notice which of the Ten Commandments Jesus cites: #5 (Honor your father and mother), #6 (Do not murder), #7 (Do not commit adultery), #8 (Do not steal), #9 (Do not give false witness), and an interesting variation on #10 (Do not covet, which Jesus enlarges here to "Love your neighbor as yourself"). These are the commandments that deal with a person's relationship to others. Commandments #1-4 deal with a person's relationship to God.

Jesus told the rich young man to be generous and he would be rewarded. Jesus invited the young man to then become a disciple. Neither of these was well received. The young man was too tied to his "stuff" to be able to turn loose of it. He held on to dirt and gave up diamonds.

Have you ever noticed that the most generous people are often the ones who appear to have the least to give? Perhaps these people aren't owned by what possessions they do have and are therefore able to turn loose of them more easily. Jesus watched one such person with great interest and we're still talking about her today:

> Jesus looked up and saw the rich putting their gifts into the offering box. He also saw a poor widow put in two small copper coins. He said, "I tell you the truth, this poor widow has put in more than all of them. For they all offered their gifts out of their wealth. But she, out of her poverty, put in everything she had to live on." (Luke 21:1-4)

Refer back to the prayer of "Confession and Pardon" referenced in the Introduction. When I read the lines, "We have not heard the cry of the needy. Forgive us, we pray", I am reminded how selfishness is an obstacle to obedience. On one of his radio shows, Chuck Swindoll said, "A life that focuses on itself will be disobedient before long. A life that focuses on Jesus Christ will be beautifully obedient."

In *Mere Christianity* (specifically, the "Social Morality" essay) C.S. Lewis wrote: "A Christian society is not going to arrive until most of us really want it, and we are not going to want it until we become fully Christian. I may repeat 'Do as you would be done by' till I am black in the face, but I cannot really carry it out till I love my neighbour as myself; and I cannot learn to love my neighbour as myself till I learn to love God; and I cannot learn to love God except by learning to obey Him."[13]

> [Jesus is speaking] "Love the Lord your God with all your heart, with all your soul, and with all your mind." This is the first and greatest commandment. The second is like it: "Love your neighbor as yourself." All the law and the prophets hang on these two commandments. (Matthew 22:37-40)

> He has told you, O man, what is proper, and what the Lord really wants from you; He wants you to promote justice, to be faithful, and *to live obediently before your God.* [emphasis added] (Micah 6:8)

> But would you like evidence, you empty person, that faith without works is useless? (James 2:20)

Paul Stallsworth made some striking points relating to obedience in one of his sermons. He said, "There is more a crisis of character than an economic crisis in this country. People are doing what they want to do to the detriment of others. Yet in exactly *this* world the Church lives as the Body of Christ." It occurred to me as I listened to this sermon that Jesus is found in joyful obedience and not in absolute freedom. Jesus *gives* absolute freedom in response to our giving Him our joyful obedience.

Greed

Greed and selfishness are opposite sides of the same coin. Selfish people won't let go of what they have and greedy people won't be content with what they have. Selfish people aren't always greedy, but greedy people are always selfish.

How often have you heard this from the pulpit: "Does your checkbook reflect your obedience to God?" Questions like this are when preachers leave preaching and go to meddling, aren't they? But sometimes we need to be reminded of this obstacle to our obedience. Psalms 119:36, 37 offers a helpful prayer: "Give me a desire for your rules, rather than wealth. Turn my eyes away from what is worthless! Revive me with your assuring word!"

Acts 5:1-10 records one of the most heartbreaking examples of greed in the Bible:

> Now a man named Ananias, together with Sapphira his wife, sold a piece of property. He kept back for himself part of the proceeds with his wife's knowledge; he brought only part of it and placed it at the apostles' feet. But Peter said, "Ananias, why has Satan filled your heart to lie to the Holy Spirit and keep back for yourself part of the proceeds from the sale of the land? Before it was sold, did it not belong to you? And when it was sold, was it not at your disposal? How have you thought up this deed in your heart? You have not lied to people but to God!"
>
> When Ananias heard these words he collapsed and died, and great fear gripped all who heard about it. So the young men came, wrapped him up, carried him out, and buried him. After

an interval of about three hours, his wife came in, but she did not know what had happened. Peter said to her, "Tell me, were the two of you paid this amount for the land?" Sapphira said, 'Yes, that much." Peter then told her, "Why have you agreed together to test the Spirit of the Lord? Look! The feet of those who have buried your husband are at the door, and they will carry you out!" At once she collapsed at his feet and died. So when the young men came in, they found her dead, and they carried her out and buried her beside her husband.

Ananias and Sapphira weren't just greedy for money. They were greedy for praise. In Acts Chapter 4 we are told about Barnabas, another disciple who sold a piece of land and gave all the money to the apostles. Probably great admiration and praise followed this generous act. Annanias and Sapphira wanted to be admired and praised, too. But they wanted it on false terms. What is so sad to me is that they would have received admiration and praise for whatever they had given. Remember 2 Corinthians 9:7? "Each one of you should give just as he has decided in his heart, not reluctantly or under compulsion, because God loves a cheerful giver." Ananias and Sapphira didn't have to lie about it. Their greed was the obstacle to their obedience.

Please don't let it be yours.

Resentment

Resentment is an acid that will consume you from the inside out. Resentful people cannot forgive and that's a huge obstacle to obedience. As Corrie ten Boom said, "Forgiveness is an act of the will—which means it requires obedience."

The book of Jonah tells the story a man consumed with resentment. It begins with a call from God to Jonah: "Go immediately to Nineveh, that large capital city, and announce judgment against its people because their wickedness has come to my attention." (Jonah 1:2)

Jonah's reaction is immediate, but it's hardly obedient: "Instead Jonah immediately headed off to a distant seaport to escape from the commission of the Lord. He traveled to Joppa and found a merchant ship heading to a distant seaport. So he paid the fare and went aboard it to go with them to a distant seaport far away from the Lord." (Jonah 1:3a)

Jonah was seriously running away from the Lord, putting more and more distance between himself and God. Or so he thought.

God used some strong discipline to get Jonah's attention. Jonah was certain he was going to die, but God delivered him. And after He did, he repeated His call: "Go immediately to Nineveh, that large city, and proclaim to it the message that I tell you." (Jonah 3:2)

This time Jonah got the message: "So Jonah went immediately to Nineveh, as the Lord had said…(Jonah 3:3a)" Jonah delivers the warning of impending judgment and to his astonishment the entire city, from the king on down, demonstrably repented and turned from their evil way of living, hoping God might be merciful. God indeed "relented concerning the judgment he had threatened them with and he did not destroy them." (Jonah 3:11)

Jonah was very angry about this. He wanted God to destroy Nineveh and he was consumed with resentment that God showed mercy to the Ninevites when they repented before Him. Remember, the people of Nineveh were Assyrians—a ruthless, bloodthirsty people who actually left monuments to

It Isn't Easy (Obstacles to Obedience)

their cruelty, torture and slaughter of people who opposed them. Israel hated and feared Nineveh with good reason. But God loved the people of Nineveh. Remember that the next time you're talking with someone who complains about how cruel the God of the Old Testament was.

The book of Jonah ends leaving the reader unsure if Jonah was ever able to let go of his resentment over God's mercy. Please don't be Jonah. Please don't let resentment stand in the way of your following God's call on your life!

Laziness

Laziness and its cousin procrastination are passive obstacles to obedience. The book of Proverbs calls the lazy person a "sluggard" and devotes numerous verses to the fate of such.

Lazy people miss out on much of life. Lazy people are very difficult to motivate, which is why laziness is an obstacle to obedience. When God called me to undertake the MS 50 Challenge Walk, laziness was not an option if I was going to be obedient to that call. Would I have preferred sleeping in on those early, early mornings? You bet I would have!

One of the worst places to see the effect of laziness is in the rearing of children. As great as the Old Testament prophet Samuel was, he was apparently a lazy parent. His sons were completely undisciplined:

> In his old age Samuel appointed his sons as judges over Israel. The name of his firstborn son was Joel, and the name of his second son was Abijah. They were judges in Beersheeba. But his sons did not follow his ways. Instead, they made money dishonestly, accepted bribes, and perverted justice. So all the elders of Israel gathered together and approached

> Samuel at Ramah. They said to him, "Look, you are old, and your sons don't follow your ways. So now appoint over us a king to lead us, just like all the nations have." (1 Samuel 8:1-5)

The irony in this is Samuel had previously seen the disaster that happened when Eli, the priest to whom he was apprenticed as a child, had failed to discipline his sons.

To be fair, perhaps Samuel wasn't lazy. Perhaps his sons were just hard-headed and rejected what he tried to teach them. But one sure way to end up with sons like Samuel's is to be a lazy parent. And look at the far-reaching impact of Samuel's sons' flagrant behavior: that was the reason the people of Israel demanded a king.

Discipline is the best cure for laziness. So if laziness is the particular obstacle to obedience with which you struggle, choose a form of discipline to follow and begin to overcome that obstacle. Remember, "So whoever knows what is good to do and does not do it is guilty of sin." (James 4:17)

Lust

The Bible has a lot to say about lust, and none of it is pretty. *The NET Bible* translator's note on Proverbs 6:25 is riveting: "Playing with temptation in the heart—the seat of the will and the emotions—is only the heart reaching out after the sin." To reach out away from God is to disobey. In contrast, to obey is to reach out for God.

King David's is one of the most graphic stories of lust in the Bible. If you need to revisit the story, it's told in 2 Samuel Chapters 11 and 12. That this story is recorded in the Scriptures at all bears witness to me of their authenticity. It was hardly David's finest hour, yet he didn't censor the sordid events being recorded. They graphically portray what James 1:15 summarizes in one sentence: "Then when desire [lust] conceives, it gives birth to sin, and when sin is full grown, it gives birth to death."

As I think about obedience, I think about the fine line that differentiates lust from longing. Lust is incredibly powerful, demanding instant gratification. Longing comes from a deeper place and generates something entirely different. I experienced that in a recent Christmas season. I find that as I've gotten older, truly there is very little in the way of "stuff" that I want—something my husband tells me makes gift-buying very difficult. One year as a particular jewelry commercial flashed a series of larger-than-life pictures on the television screen, one ring in particular literally took my breath away with its beauty. I lusted for that ring. In truth I did not need or want the ring—my fingers are quite adequately covered with rings that hold deep meaning for me. But the desire I felt to possess *that* particular ring was lust in its purest form—sharp, intense, immediate, almost suffocatingly consuming. I went to the jewelry store to look at it and try it on. It was even more beautiful in person than it had been in the picture.

By contrast, within a day or two of my seeing the jewelry commercial, my husband and I were shopping for gifts for our grandson. We walked around the shopping center, visiting various stores just to see what they offered. One store we visited sold sea shells. Inside one of the glass display cases I saw a large, magnificent shell that took my breath away with its beauty, just as the ring had done a few days earlier. Seeing that shell awoke in me a deep longing. I remembered regularly visiting the local shell shop when I was a child and how much I admired all the large beautiful shells. How I wished I could afford to buy one! I longed for an amazingly beautiful shell, also known as a "jewel shell."

I recognized there was a difference between how I felt about the beautiful ring and how I felt about the beautiful shell. I lusted for the ring, but I longed for the shell. I asked for, and to my joy received, the shell (not the ring) for Christmas. Each day I see it and admire the incredible beauty of God's creation in every exquisite detail. You see, God created that shell and there isn't another shell exactly like it anywhere. A person created the ring, although admittedly with talent God gave. About a month after I first saw a picture of the ring, I realized I hadn't thought about it for many days. The emotional intensity had completely faded and I no longer wanted to possess it at all. Like all other lusts, this lust—when ignored—faded away. However, the longing, fully satisfied, still brings real joy and thanksgiving.

In the context of obedience I see it's important to be able to distinguish between lust and longing, so I can know what to obey for my own good. The Scriptures speak of our longing for God and warn against the lust of our hearts. Lust is far too immediate and transitory an emotion to allow us the luxury of time to think about it, to assess it, to evaluate it. Lust is transitory. Longing implies a long time to fulfill.

Grief

Grief can be every bit as debilitating as fear. I remember the immediate aftermath of my father's suicide, when grief completely consumed me. I couldn't even find the energy to water my plants. I would look out the window at them and think, "I don't care if you die. I'm too numb to move."

Where does obedience come into play when our personal world stops turning? That's a hard one. But it begins with our prayer admitting we need God's help. We cannot receive unless and until we ask. Not long after my father's death, I was at home alone and in deep despair. Angrily I yelled at God, "You promised peace. Remember? 'Peace I give you,

My peace I leave you.' Well, *where is it?*" Almost immediately I fell asleep on the sofa. While I was asleep I had an incredible dream, a dream I know—absolutely, unequivocally *know*—came straight from the Lord. The last words I heard before I woke up were, "Be patient. You will be all right eventually." That may not sound like much comfort, but it was everything I needed to hear at that moment. It was a promise I could hold onto.

In one of the most memorable sermons I've ever heard, Paul Stallsworth said, "Faith is not a noun but rather an action verb; we are given faith in order to *do* something. Faith that moves us to reach out and share each other's troubles and problems is truly an obedient faith. We were never meant to be a people in isolation." As one of my best friends says, "to be alone inside my own head is to be in enemy territory."

Losses are an inevitable part of our lives. We must mourn and deeply grieve our losses before we can heal. I remember the time I spent with a godly counselor as I struggled with the many unmourned losses of my own life. I see now that even mourning, when done with God's loving help, is an act of obedience. And yes, joy and peace are also attainable during periods of grief and mourning. Joy and peace in the midst of tears are possible through a relationship with Jesus Christ and the hope of what is to come.

Stubbornness/Rebellion

I still remember the first time someone called me a rebel. Along with three co-workers, I was attending specialty training out of state. One night in the recreation center I was shooting pool with the instructor when he casually asked, "How long have you been a rebel?" I was surprised by the question. I'm the person who follows the rules, who doesn't like to make waves.

"I'm not a rebel," I replied.

"Yes you are," he persisted. "I watch all the students when they arrive, because I learn useful things about them before class even starts. Typically people attending in a group sit together. When your group walked in, you sat on the opposite side of the room from your colleagues. That tells me you're a rebel. A quiet rebel, but a rebel nonetheless."

You know something? He was right. I have always been an avowed nonconformist in many areas, and I can be very stubborn.

Is there any better example in the Bible of stubbornness and rebellion than the Israelites after their deliverance from Egypt? The Israelites' persistent rebellion caused God to frequently refer to them as a "stubborn and stiff-necked people." One of the most stubbornly rebellious things the Israelites did was to persistently worship idols. God had some pointed words about that: "Certainly, obedience is better than sacrifice; paying attention is better than the fat of rams. For rebellion is like the sin of divination, and presumption is like the evil of idolatry." (1 Samuel 15:22b, 23a)

When the Scripture says stubbornness is as bad as worshiping idols, it means you have made an idol out of yourself. When I refuse to obey God because it conflicts with what I want at the moment, I'm saying my will is much more important than God's will. If I persist in this attitude, I am not just being rebellious; I am being stubborn. I have set myself and my desires up as a personal idol, and God warns that is not an acceptable position to take. Indeed, it is a perilous position, one I would be best advised to give up quickly. Throughout Scripture we see that the one thing God absolutely will not tolerate is idolatry. He will not share us with anyone or anything else.

It Isn't Easy (Obstacles to Obedience)

Have you noticed that when the Israelites persistently rebelled against God in the desert, God left them to their own resources? And when they realized how difficult life without God was, they returned to God, Whom they found waiting. What a powerful image of the simplicity and challenge of obedience!

During a sermon on the Trinity, Steve Castle said, "We part ways with the road called obedience when it forks in a direction we don't like. Obedience is an act of will, pure and simple. Joyful obedience is relational; there is no obedience without trust. We're not to have a blind faith but to use our mind." Which caused me to wonder: Jesus is perfectly trustworthy, so why is obedience so hard when it should be a joyful journey?

I think our stubbornness and rebellion are rooted in our pride. Milton wrote how Satan preferred ruling in hell to serving in heaven. Too often we act as if we believe that, too. We cannot be obedient when we insist on having everything our way. In one particular sermon, Paul Stallsworth talked about healing and obedience. He made a challenging, even shocking assertion: "Today mental illness is often another word for stubbornness." Having had a family member who suffered through mental illness, Paul had a basis for his particular insight.

Stubbornness and rebellion loom large when it comes to the political structure of a nation. There are times when obedience to the government becomes very, very difficult and it is hard to read the following verses of Scripture:

> For there is no authority except by God's appointment, and the authorities that exist have been instituted by God…Therefore it is necessary to be in subjection, not only because of the wrath of the

> authorities but also because of your conscience. Romans 13:1b, 5)
>
> Remind them to be subject to rulers and authorities, to be obedient, to be ready for every good work. They must not slander anyone, but be peaceable, gentle, showing complete courtesy to all people.(Titus 3:1, 2)
>
> Arrogant people do nothing but scoff at me, yet I do not turn aside from your law. (Psalms 119:51)

May God give all of us the grace we need to live out the challenge of these verses and to know how to apply them! After all, what if Joseph had not been obedient to Caesar Augustus' despised census mandate requiring him to travel to Bethlehem with Mary to be registered for taxes? Jesus would not have been born in Bethlehem in fulfillment of the prophecy!

That said, it is also important for us to remember that there will be times when, "We must obey God rather than men" (Acts 5:29). As Proverbs 28:4 says, "Those who forsake the law praise the wicked, but those who keep the law contend with them."

There is a vast difference between being stubbornly obedient to God and being stubbornly disobedient to God. It is imperative we know—and live—the difference.

Impatience

To be obedient means we must also be patient at times and to wait for the promise to be fulfilled in our own lives. Advent is a wonderful season for practicing patience. As with the beginning of Mary's pregnancy, it seems nothing is happening at all. It is a time of waiting on God to fulfill what He has promised.

Impatience causes much of the trouble in our lives. I think Judas betrayed Jesus in part because he was impatient. Judas was tired of waiting for the Messiah to overthrow the power of Rome.

Impatience reveals itself to us in the way we drive, the way we wait in line, and the way we wait, period. Perfect patience pursues the right thing at the right time in the right way.

Henri Nouwen wrote an Advent meditation titled, "Waiting Patiently Means 'Living the Present Moment'." In it he wrote, "Waiting patiently always means paying attention to what is happening right before our eyes and seeing there the first rays of God's glorious coming." Reading this reminded me of the time I was in Bermuda and decided to get up early and watch the sun rise over the ocean. It was pitch black as I made my way to the side of the cliff; the stars were so bright and full—completely different from what I normally see at home, where man-made lights infringe on the darkness. I watched as the horizon began to brighten. But the process was slow, maddeningly slow, so much so that after what seemed hours of waiting I actually said to myself, "I'm tired of this; I'm leaving. The sun just isn't coming up today." (Yes, I really did say that!) At that exact moment, I saw the first gleam of sunlight pierce the horizon and heard God's amused voice say to me, "Oh, really?" I agree with Nouwen; to be obedient is to wait patiently, paying attention indeed to what is happening right before our eyes.

Before you think I have somehow arrived in the patience department, let me tell you about the day my morning prayer was for God to give me the grace to live out that one day in joyful obedience. I came close. But when our church women's group had to wait while the restaurant prepared the room for our evening Christmas party, I grumbled needlessly at the wait. Yet I had still made progress—I actually recognized, and asked forgiveness for, my impatience!

Ingratitude

Shakespeare wrote the following words in his play, *King Lear*: "How sharper than a serpent's tooth it is to have an ungrateful child!" If you are a parent, have you ever felt that way? If you're not a parent (or even if you are), have you ever caused your parents to feel that way? Have you ever caused God—your heavenly parent—to feel that way?

Ingratitude is an ugly thing. At the Community Thanksgiving Gathering in our town one year, Steve Castle gave the sermon. And, although the topic ("What Better Reason Do You Need") was on thanksgiving and gratitude, obedience was underneath it all. Following are some of Steve's observations:

- Why do we celebrate Thanksgiving only one day out of the year?

- In Luke 12:15, Jesus said, "one's life does not consist in the abundance of his possessions", yet our culture says otherwise. Why do we listen to the culture?

- Why can't we be happy with what we have, with what God gives us?

- We have RHS, Restless Heart Syndrome, always longing for more than we have. It's difficult to be thankful when you have RHS. RHS keeps us from being obedient to our Lord. God intends for us to be discontented with some things, but we flip-flop it—we try to fill the God void with the "stuff".

- It is right to be contented with what we have but not with who we are. Isn't it time to stop wailing because "it isn't good enough", and start being thankful it's not what we deserve?

- Let's work on ourselves to be thankful in all circumstances.

- Why not ask how long this stuff we want will make us happy?

- Why not cultivate a grateful heart?

- Where does my soul find true satisfaction?

Most of my answers to Steve's questions were: "Because we're disobedient. Let's be obedient for a change." There is a definite connection between gratitude and obedience. Grateful people "get it." Ungrateful people don't. You can see this very clearly in Luke 17:11-19:

> Now on the way to Jerusalem Jesus was passing along between Samaria and Galilee. As he was entering a village, he was met by ten men with leprosy. They stood at a distance, raised their voices and said, "Jesus, Master, have mercy on us." When he saw them he said, "Go and show yourselves to the priests." And as they went along, they were cleansed. Then one of them, when he saw he was healed, turned back, praising God with a loud voice. He fell with his face to the ground at Jesus' feet and thanked him. (Now he was a Samaritan.) Then Jesus said, 'Were not ten cleansed? Where are the other nine? Was no one found to turn back and give praise to God except this foreigner?" Then he said to the man, "Get up and go your way. Your faith has made you well."

Ten men in desperate need of healing reached out to Jesus for help. Outcast because of their leprosy, these were men whom no one would touch or even come near. Ten men whose lives had no purpose or meaning reached out to Jesus and Jesus reached back in a miraculous way. Only one of the men was truly grateful, though and he happened to be a Samaritan. This man stopped in his tracks when he realized he was healed and he turned back to show his gratitude to Jesus. The ingratitude of the nine children of Abraham, the nine chosen people of God, was not lost on Jesus. He even pointed it out to those around Him.

We need to be the tenth leper.

I remember the interview I had for the last job I held before opening my own business. When my future boss asked me about my work philosophy, I told him, "I want to do my job so well that when you wake up every morning and look at yourself in the mirror while you're shaving, you tell yourself, 'I'm so glad I hired her.'" Can you tell I was grateful for the opportunity I was at that point hoping to have? When was the last time you were grateful for the work you do?

At a recent Wednesday evening service, Karl Zorowski delivered a breathtaking sermon on gratitude. He began by talking about how fervent and detailed the prayers are in the waiting room of a hospital while a loved one is undergoing a surgical procedure. He talked about the profound relief that is felt by the family when the doctor finally comes out and says, "Everything went well, she's going to be just fine." Then he asked, "Where's the gratitude to God for the answered prayer? Why don't we kneel and give thanks with the same level of fervor we showed when we knelt to pray our original request for healing? Why don't we pray after the surgery: 'Thank you, Lord, for the skill of the anesthesiologist, thank you for guiding the hands of the surgeon, thank you for the attentiveness of the nurses?"

When was the last time you expressed your gratitude to God? If you are having difficulty being obedient to God, perhaps your ingratitude has become an obstacle.

****

You see how easily obstacles to obedience can cause us to stumble and fall? It occurs to me we often choose vice over virtue because we think virtue requires us to give up things we might otherwise want to do. However, virtue is not the tyrannical joy-killer we make it out to be. I think what we dislike about virtue is the element of obedience that underlies it. Consider the four Cardinal virtues of Prudence, Temperance, Justice, and Fortitude. To successfully possess any of them requires obedience to something outside ourselves and our own desires. Again, the Scriptures give insight into how we should proceed:

> We will obey what the Lord our God to whom
> we are sending you tells us to do. It doesn't
> matter whether we like what he tells us or not.
> We will obey what he tells us to do so that
> things will go well for us. (Jeremiah 42:6)

> Although he was a son, he learned obedience
> through the things he suffered. (Hebrews 5:8)

Perhaps this is the true reason why we despise obedience. To obey is also to deny. It means denying ourselves and our preferred choices. Obeying means to give up doing whatever we want, whenever we want, however we want, and to do that *is* to suffer in a very real sense.

How, then, can we ever hope to get to a point where obedience is "joyful"?

> For it is written: "You are to worship the Lord your God and serve only Him". (Matthew 4:10b)
>
> If you continue to follow my teaching, you are really my disciples and you will know the truth, and the truth will set you free. (John 8:31, 32)
>
> Keep his commandments very carefully, as well as the stipulations and statutes he commanded you to do. Do whatever is proper and good before the Lord so that it may go well with you. (Deuteronomy 6:17, 18a)
>
> ...so that the righteous requirements of the law may be fulfilled in us, who do not walk according to the flesh but according to the Spirit. (Romans 8:4)
>
> I also call on you to love the Lord your God, to obey him and cling to him, for he is your life and the means of your longevity. (Deuteronomy 30:20a)

The answer is as easy as it is difficult. We worship, we praise, we cling to, and we choose God. As we do, we become closer to God and we grow in our love to the point where we want God's will more than we want the air we breathe. Joyful obedience is only possible through a living relationship with Jesus Christ as Lord, with the Holy Spirit firmly in control of our hearts.

The secret to victory comes through obedience.

CHAPTER 7

Warning: God Responds to Disobedience

Although disobedience was the first active sin of mankind, it was motivated by the sin of Pride ("You can be just like God if you do this!") While Pride was the thought, disobedience was the action. So disobedience has shadowed Pride ever since. Any time we succumb to Pride, disobedience is soon to follow.

Have you ever stopped to think that obedience is only possible when the opportunity for disobedience exists? Obedience, then, is a true test of our free will. People who feel no need to obey soon discover they cannot obey, and therefore they never discover the need for repentance, conversion, and transformation.

When God created Adam and Eve and placed them in the Garden of Eden, there was only one opportunity for active disobedience (i.e., sin of commission)—eating the fruit of the one tree that was prohibited. Anything else would have been passive disobedience (i.e., a sin of omission), like neglecting to care for the garden or the creatures. You get the impression from reading the Genesis account that this wasn't even a remote possibility, that Adam and Eve lived together with God in such complete and joyous harmony that their assigned work wasn't work, it was a delight. To not care for creation would never have occurred to them, even as a fleeting thought. Our parents understood all the nuances of joyful obedience with which we—I—struggle today.

When you get right down to it, there aren't really that many things in our own lives to which God says, "No". In each and every case, God's "No" involves something that isn't good for us. Like a loving parent, God has the long view of life—the really, really long view of life. As in *eternity*.

Active disobedience—sins of commission—can be summed up in three short sentences:

1. I saw it.
2. I wanted it.
3. I took it.

When God asked Eve to account for her actions, she said in effect, "I saw the fruit and it looked good; I wanted it so I could be wise; therefore I took it and ate it." Note the I—I—I there. Not, "I saw the fruit and wanted it, so I asked God for it." Not, "I saw the fruit and wanted it, so I asked God to help me get it." No, it was "I saw the fruit, I wanted the fruit, I took and ate the fruit. I didn't care what God or anyone else thought." We've been rationalizing our wants like that ever since. Look at one example:

Most of the time, people get into debt because, "I saw it, I wanted it, but I didn't have the money so I bought it with my credit card (never mind that I can't afford it)." Or as Dave Ramsey often puts it, "people say 'I deserve it because I breathe air'." Our country has a problem with chronic obesity, which often can be summarized by, "I saw the candy bar, I wanted the candy bar, I ate the candy bar."

Many of you reading this are familiar with Jeremiah 29:11: "For I know what I have planned for you," says the Lord. "For I have plans to prosper you, not to harm you. I have plans to give you a future filled with hope."

Did you notice the Lord speaks of plans—plural—and not plan, singular? It seems God is prepared for our failures. Leslie Weatherhead, in his book *The Will of God*, said God's will is three-fold: Intentional, Circumstantial, and Ultimate.

Whether we know it or not, we start life with God's intentional plan for us; it's the way God wants us to go. However, as Karl Zorowski says, "Evil happens when God's will is thwarted by human disobedience." That's when God's circumstantial will kicks in to take us where God's ultimate will wants us to be. Weatherhead asserts that *nothing* can thwart the ultimate will of God.

I find it hugely comforting to know God prepares multiple plans for us because He already knows we will not be obedient. Just as a parent knows what a child will do because the parent knows the character of that child, so God knows our character better than we can ever hope to ourselves. But even so, obedience is not impossible. It is a matter of choice, a choice that carries consequences with it:

> Do you not know that if you present yourselves as obedient slaves, you are slaves of the one you obey, either of sin resulting in death, or obedience resulting in righteousness? (Romans 6:16)

> The one who despises instruction will pay the penalty, but whoever esteems instruction will be rewarded. (Proverbs 13:13)

> Notice therefore the kindness and harshness of God—harshness toward those who have fallen, but God's kindness towards you, provided you continue in his kindness; otherwise, you also will be cut off. (Romans 11:22)

> They quickly turned aside from the path their ancestors had walked. Their ancestors had obeyed the Lord's commands, but they did not. (Judges 2:17b)

> He left those nations simply because he wanted to teach the subsequent generations of Israelites, who had not experienced the earlier battles…These…nations…were left to test Israel, so the Lord would know if his people would obey the commands he gave their ancestors through Moses. (Judges 3:2-4)
>
> But whoever obeys his word, truly in this person the love of God has been perfected. By this we know that we are in him. (1 John 2:5)

The hardest truth for me to accept is that my disobedience has brought most of the misery in my life. But my greatest comfort is that I do not have to remain there!

Dr. Charles Stanley has said, "Disobedience blocks God's blessing. It's very important to obey in the little things He tells you to do. Here's the tragedy of disobeying God: If you don't obey in something simple you may never find your calling in life. Too often our response is we're too busy doing (fill in whatever it is we're putting before God at the moment)." Hearing this reminds me whenever I put my own interests before those of God, I have created an idol and used it to disobey. And once again I see that the only way to clearly understand what it is God expects from me is to pay attention to Him and to His Word. I cannot obey what I do not know, and yet God does not hold me blameless for disobeying things I should know but have stubbornly refused to know. As Romans 1:20 states, "For since the creation of the world his invisible attributes—his eternal power and divine nature—have been clearly seen, because they are understood through what has been made. So people are without excuse."

One morning on *Dr. James Dobson's Family Talk* radio program, I caught a portion of a talk by Dr. Dorothy

Patterson. Using the Genesis account of Adam and Eve, she described four steps that descend into disobedience:

1. We contradict God ("Did God really say not to eat of the fruit?")
2. We disagree with God ("No, God didn't really mean that.")
3. We supersede God ("I've got a better idea.")
4. We disobey God ("I'm going to do it.")

The point that struck me was we don't begin at the point of disobedience. We get there gradually, led astray by our desire to have our own preferences. Again, that speaks of why Jesus Christ must free us for joyful obedience. There simply is no way we can get there on our own abilities.

Rest assured, God *does* respond to our disobedience. He loves us too much not to. When we, like a stubborn child, insist on our "Yes" where God says "No", God responds to our defiance. The mercy of God cannot be separated from the judgment of God. Our increasingly soft, comfort-loving culture seems to have forgotten this unpleasant truth. We love mercy and endless second chances—especially where we're concerned—and we think judgment is harsh and outdated and not really necessary. Somewhere along the way we've lost our understanding of what sin is.

When reading the Scriptures, I see only two ways God responds to our disobedience: discipline or abandonment.

Discipline

Scripture gives many illustrations of the tragedy that occurs when "I saw, I wanted, I took" happen inside the strength of our own will. Note that in every case, the person does not confess the deed until *after* being confronted about it:

- In 1 Samuel Chapter 10, King Saul was waiting for Samuel to arrive and offer the sacrifice. When Samuel took longer than expected, Saul saw his men becoming restless; wanting to be successful in the battle, he took the sacrifice and offered it himself. That led to his losing God's guidance and eventually the kingdom.

- In 2 Samuel Chapter 11, King David was lounging around the palace when he was supposed to be on the battlefield. He saw Bathsheba, he wanted her, and he ordered her brought to him. That supposedly private sin led to murder, death, and bloody rebellion from within his own family.

- In 1 Kings Chapter 21, King Ahab saw the vineyard of his next-door neighbor and wanted it for a vegetable garden. When the neighbor refused to sell it (the refusal was in accordance with Jewish law), Ahab's wife Jezebel took it for him by having the neighbor framed and murdered.

God applies discipline according to the level of our disobedience. If we persist in disobeying, God will increase the pressure on us, raising our level of discomfort in an effort to get our attention. God really doesn't want to give up on us.

However—and this, to me, is a truly terrifying thought—we can disobey God beyond the point of His discipline. We can stubbornly disobey God to the point where He will leave us completely alone with the consequences of our actions. If we persistently refuse to repent, God can, and will, abandon us.

Abandonment

The parable of the prodigal son in Luke 15:11-32 tells of a father who loved his son too much to rescue him from his consequences. Even when the son is at the point of starvation, the father didn't rescue him. The father in effect abandoned his son for the young man's own good. But the father waited and watched for the first sign of the son's return and repentance, and his immediate response was to throw a huge party celebrating his safe return.

The Israelites went into captivity and exile because of their repeated disobedience. God finally stopped disciplining them and abandoned them to their enemies. But God never stopped loving them. God never stopped waiting for them to come to their senses and turn around. God never stopped trying to get their attention, reminding them how much better life had been—and would be again—when they lived as the children of a loving Father.

Perhaps the hardest account of abandonment to read is the one that followed Achan's sin in Joshua Chapter 7. This very difficult passage is important because Achan's sin is about much more than the far-reaching consequences of one person's sin. It is about the holiness of God and the necessity of God's judgment, from which great good can come.

Let's review the events leading up to Achan's sin:

God had told the Israelites to enter and take the Promised Land. In Numbers 13:26-33, ten of the twelve returning spies made a report that terrified the people so much they refused to go forward. In Numbers Chapter 14, God told the people as a consequence of their unbelief and disobedience they would wander in the wilderness until all those who rebelled had died. The next morning, the people told Moses in effect, "We were wrong yesterday, and we're sorry; today we're ready to do what God told us to do." Moses replied by telling them it was too late. (Just the thought of ever hearing God say, "It's too late" terrifies me!)

Forty years later, Joshua succeeded Moses as the new leader of the Israelites, who crossed the Jordan on dry land, just as their parents crossed the Red Sea on dry land. This allowed a new generation to see God was still at work in their lives. The people know what God demands and they've agreed to follow the Law. They are not surprised when God tells them, "All the silver and gold, as well as bronze and iron items, belong to the Lord." (Joshua 6:19a) Jericho is the first conquest they will make, and this directive is simply a continuation of the principle of first fruits.

However, Joshua Chapter 7 records a man named Achan decides to disobey God. Although a wealthy man, when he sees a fancy robe he likes and some gold and silver, Achan decides to take them. (Note the "I saw, I wanted, I took" principle at work here.) Achan knows what he's done is wrong, as shown by his hiding the items under the floor in his tent. Apparently his children also know what he's done and collude with him to hide what he's taken. It's a private family sin that no one knows about, right? Wrong. God knows.

When Achan decided to take some of the plunder he effectively thumbed his nose at God. Plunder was, after all, the normal course of war. When you saw something you liked and you wanted it, you took it. But the Mosaic law gave specific rules even for plunder. It was not to be a random, thoughtless process. And the specific requirement to refrain from plunder this one particular time was about the holiness of God.

For God to overlook Achan's sin of disobedience, especially at this stage of the nation's formation, was to set in motion the sure destruction of Israel. After all, if God wasn't really serious about this order, then He probably wasn't all that serious about the rest of His laws either, so why bother to pay attention to them—or to God, for that matter.

Joshua only learned of Achan's sin when Israel lost its second battle with a much smaller city. When he asked God for an explanation, God replied Israel had sinned by taking forbidden plunder and He was no longer going to be with them. He was abandoning them to their enemies. The secret sin of one man was laid on the entire nation, because God knew that it would spread like an infection if not stopped. What would happen next was up to Joshua.

Achan, when finally cornered, admits what he did. (Warning: an admission of guilt when you're caught red-handed is not the same thing as confession and repentance!)

The penalty was swift and it seems brutally harsh: Achan and his entire family were put to death by the community as community reparation for community sin against the holiness of God. It was sin that required judgment for the good of the entire nation to avert their total destruction.

Again, this is a very hard story to read; it is especially difficult to read from the perspective of today's culture. But while Scripture is often comforting, it is not soft. We try to tone it down at our own peril.

But abandonment by God can get much worse. God can abandon us to ourselves. Romans 1:24 begins, "Therefore God gave them over in the desires of their hearts to impurity"; Romans 1:26 continues, "For this reason God gave them over to dishonorable passions"; and in Romans 1:28 we read, "And just as they did not see fit to acknowledge God, God gave them over to a depraved mind, to do what should not be done." Romans 1:29-32 continues with a list of the consequences of a depraved mind.

As terrible as being abandoned to ourselves would be, there is one even more terrible abandonment from which there can be no recovery: Hell. Although hell is the ultimate abandonment by God, hell is not imposed upon us by God. Hell is chosen by us, much to God's heartbreak and sorrow. The Apostle Peter wrote: "The Lord is not slow concerning his promise, as some regard slowness, but is being patient toward you, because he does not wish for any to perish but for all to come to repentance." (2 Peter 3:9)

In David Gregory's exceptional book, *Dinner with a Perfect Stranger*, he tells the fictional story of a young man invited to dinner with Jesus Christ. At one point during the dinner the young man, who doesn't believe he's really having dinner with Jesus and thinks he's been "pranked" by his friends, asks Jesus if hell really exists. Jesus replies in the affirmative and tells him, "You don't want to be there." When the young man presses for an explanation, Jesus asks him to think of every good thing he's ever experienced in his life and then says, "It's not there." What a perfect description of hell.

Please, please, please. Don't be there. No level of disobedience is worth it. If persistent disobedience in some area of your life is consuming you, turn around before it's too late.

Remember, no one becomes like God by disobeying God. Adam and Eve tried it and failed miserably. The most beautiful angel in all creation tried it and became the devil.

CHAPTER 8

The Divine Rewards of Obedience

The rewards of obedience aren't counted in the currency of this world. Rather, they are divine in nature and include salvation, eternal life, being filled with the Holy Spirit, true discipleship, wisdom, blessings from God, fulfillment, rest and peace, security, the best life has to offer, restoration of divine innocence, joy, closeness to God, friendship with Jesus. Let's look at a few of those in more detail.

Hebrews 5:5-10 has an interesting take on the rewards of obedience that Jesus Christ experienced:

> So also Christ did not glorify himself in becoming high priest, but the one who glorified him was God, who said to him, "You are my son! Today I have fathered you," as also in another place God says, "You are a priest forever in the order of Melchizedek." During his earthly life Christ offered both requests and supplications, with loud cries and tears, to the one who was able to save him from death and he was heard because of his devotion. Although he was a son, he learned obedience through the things he suffered. And by being perfected in this way, he became the source of eternal salvation to all who obey him, and he was designated by God as high priest in the order of Melchizedek.

Notice it is through Jesus Christ's obedience that He becomes the source of our salvation. Did you ever consider that your salvation is His reward for obedience?

But salvation also begins with our obedience—saying "yes"—to God's gracious invitation of eternal life through Jesus Christ. While this surely is more than enough reward to make obedience worthwhile, God has so much more planned for us. If you're a fan of C.S. Lewis' The Chronicles of Narnia series, you'll recognize when I quote Repicheep from *The Last Battle*, "Come further up and further in."[14]

It seems obedience is not part of being Christian. It's *everything* about being Christian. Christ is the source of salvation only to those who obey Him. We have to turn from our disobedience and towards Him before we can accept salvation. Really, it isn't all that complicated. And yes, as simple as it is, it can still be so hard to grasp.

For me, the greatest act of obedience in the Bible was recorded in Luke 23:32-43, in the account of the thief on the cross. Consider the situation from the perspective of the thief: if ever a man looked less like a king, it was Jesus on the cross—beaten almost beyond recognition, abandoned by most of his followers, mocked by the general populace, utterly helpless and dying.

Matthew's gospel (Matthew 27:44) records, "The robbers who were crucified with him also spoke abusively to him." I confess there have been times in my life when I sought to relieve my own pain by hurling insults at someone else. Trying vainly to bring myself up by tearing someone else down never worked, though. It only made me feel worse.

Incredibly, in that dark, desperate situation, Grace broke in on one of the two criminals. It first showed itself in his taking responsibility for his own life's actions: "for we are getting what we deserve for what we did" (Luke 23:41a). Next he defended Jesus, saying, "but this man has done nothing wrong" (Luke 23:41b). Then, in a truly astounding expression of faith, the dying thief turns to Jesus with a compelling request: "Jesus, remember me when you come in your kingdom" (Luke 23:42).

Have you ever stopped to consider the situation from Jesus' perspective? Only a week before, the crowds had thrown palm branches before Him, shouting loud praises. Now He is alone. Except for His mother, a few other women, and John, his followers have run away in fear for their own lives. All He hears is mocking and cursing. He is moments from what He knows will be truly terrible aloneness—when God Himself will turn away from Him. Think of the sorrow in His soul that was even deeper than the sorrow in His body.

Then, amazingly, imagine yourself in that situation hearing someone actually defend you to another. Even more amazingly, imagine hearing someone say in effect, "I believe you are a king and are going to your kingdom." What would your response be to his request that you remember him when you reach that kingdom? When Jesus said, "I tell you the truth, today you will be with me in paradise" (Luke 23:43), I think He couldn't wait to introduce this man to his Father!

Jesus' experience with the robber who defended him resonates with me on a very personal level. I was severely bullied as a child, and at a parochial school, no less! No one took my side when I was tormented. It was a miserable time in my life, and more often than not I was in tears when my mother picked me up at the end of the day. All that changed in a single instant when I was in fifth grade. The teacher was called out of the room, which meant our class sergeant-at-arms, Mike Burns was in charge. Protocol required a student to raise their hand and be acknowledged before speaking. My chief tormentor raised her hand and requested permission to speak. I could tell from the way she looked at me that I was about to be in for some major abuse, and I braced myself for the pain of it. Imagine my shock to hear Mike say, "Not if it's about Patti." I don't know who was more shocked, me or my

Obedience: The Joyful Discipline?

tormentor. But I do know the immense gratitude I felt to Mike on so many levels. His defense of me that day marked a change in how others also treated me.

Another view of divine rewards for obedience came from Keith Tonkel, a much beloved former pastor of ours. Keith often said that the reward for living a Christian life will be having lived a Christian life. We glorify the Lord when we obey Him, and we see the miracles of His presence. When we obey God, we experience the blessings of the Holy Spirit, Who fills our lives and empowers us to do things we never dreamed possible. This can include changing another person's life.

In a previous professional career, I worked with a fellow believer who was closer to me than my own brothers. One day I was almost overwhelmed by a firm prompt from the Holy Spirit to tell this man God wanted him to change careers and become a priest. I resisted just as firmly, protesting on several levels. I pointed out to God that I was not about to tell someone else what to do with his life, especially something that would sound so absurd and make me look ridiculous. The prompt persisted, more firmly. Finally, with pounding heart and a dry throat, I approached my friend and said, "I am not in the habit of telling people what to do with their lives, but I will have no peace from the Lord until I tell you that He wants you to become a priest."

I braced for his laughter—his girlfriend, after all, was a good friend of mine—but I was not at all prepared for the very strange look that came over his face. "Interesting," he said. "I've been feeling that same call. In fact, I have an appointment with the bishop to discuss it later this week."

Steve Castle, in preaching from Matthew 25:31-26, said, "The Christian life never finds its fulfillment in one's own worship or one's own piety, but in the obedient service of others. The *byproduct* of obedience is to become true disciples of Jesus Christ. Through the power of serving others God transforms us. The nature of our discipleship reflects how we view the Lord Jesus Christ."

Sometimes the closeness to God we experience as a reward for obedience comes during the journey itself, much like the disciples on the road to Emmaus experienced.

Consider some lessons from the journey God called Abram to undertake. Although God didn't give Abram a road map for the journey, He did promise to show Abram where to go. So Abram was exercising trusting obedience, believing the outcome would be good for him. As the psalmist wrote: "Tell me where you want me to go and I will go there. May every fiber of my being unite in reverence to Your name." (Psalms 86:11, 12)

Consider these points as well:

- If Abram had not been obedient to God's call, where would salvation be today?

- If we're obedient it will make a difference to the world down the road. We may not see the end, but we will see the beginning. God didn't promise Abram one single thing when He called him at first.

- Abram does what God asks him to do. It isn't until Abram *responds* that the covenant begins. Later (Joshua 3:15 and following), the Jordan doesn't part until the priests begin and take the first step.

- When we're obedient, God continues to pour out His promises and blessings to us. Remember Job

> 42:10, where Job's life didn't turn around until *after* he obeyed God and prayed for his critical, unsympathetic friends?

- God is always looking for something new to do in us if we only are obedient and get on the road again.

God often calls us to journey out into the unknown, the same way He did Abram. It seems God sends us out, but He does not promise where the journey will end, only that it will be a good thing.

> The Lord is both kind and fair; that is why he teaches sinners the right way to live. May he show the humble what is right! May he teach the humble his way! The Lord always proves faithful and reliable to those who follow the demands of his covenant. (Psalms 25:8-10)

> The one who deals wisely in a matter will find success, and blessed is the one who trusts in the Lord. (Proverbs 16:20)

I once joined my best friend on an unexpected journey of obedient faith. Dolly's house had been broken into and robbed while her three children were home after school. They had called her at work to tell her what was happening. Fortunately the robber did not harm the children, but he fled before the police arrived. Among the things he stole was her late mother's wedding ring. The police told her they knew who had done it, but did not have the evidence needed to arrest the man.

One day she called me and said, "God has put it on my heart that I need to face this man and tell him I forgive him. Will you go with me?" I sensed God telling me to go, so I agreed.

We met at her house, prayed together, anointed each other with oil, and walked down the street to the housing project where the man lived.

Dolly knocked on his door and a woman opened it. She inquired if he was in and the woman, who said she was his sister, said he was not (although we had reason to believe he was). Dolly asked her to give him a message. She said, "I just wanted to tell him I forgive him and to thank him for not being the kind of person who would harm my children. He can keep the stuff." The sister nodded emphatically and said, "No, he wouldn't ever hurt children." We said goodbye and walked back to her house, praising God the entire way. As a side note, our pastor almost had a heart attack when we shared this at the weekly prayer meeting!

While God certainly blesses obedience, sometimes blessings bring problems. In a sermon based on Genesis 13, Steve Castle talked about the account of Abram and Lot parting ways to avoid conflict. He pointed out:

- Blessings can bring problems when there is abundance. Abram took the high road and ended up with the greater blessing.

- The difference between Lot and Abram is Abram continually worships God and gives thanks every step along the way. Abram knew who God was and he worshipped God wherever he was. Who and why we worship is more important than where.

I found an important cautionary note in this sermon: if our obedience is indeed the prerequisite for the abundance of blessings God desires to give us, we need to also be keenly aware of and prepared to respond to the problems that are likely to follow. When we're not expecting problems—

especially those problems caused by the blessings of obedience—the unexpected stress and trauma they bring can easily derail the very obedience that led to them in the first place. We can also quickly forget to worship and give thanks when we're mired in the midst of problems. But in these situations, we still need to hold fast to obedience. Many of God's promises are conditional upon our actions, just as some of them are conditional upon our refraining from certain actions: "But in the same way every faithful promise the Lord your God made to you has been realized, it is just as certain, if you disobey, that the Lord will bring on you every judgment until he destroys you from this good land which the Lord your God gave you." (Joshua 23:15)

One day I was listening to Dr. Charles Stanley on the radio as I was driving to work and his message on the rewards of obedience was so powerful I had to pull off the road and take notes. The following are the excerpts that spoke so powerfully to me:

- If we focus on doing what everyone is doing in the world around us, we won't obey God very often.

- Every time God tells you to do something, He has something good in store for you. You can't wait for the big events; it's obedience in the little things. What's the last little thing God asked you to do that you haven't done?

- Jesus never forgets anything but our sin. You cannot obey God without being blessed. Jesus honored Peter's simple obedience of making his fishing boat available. What do you have that is not available to Jesus Christ? How many times have we missed a fantastic blessing because what we have is not available?

- I have obeyed God at times when I didn't see what I wanted at the time, but later I realized it was just what I wanted.

Obedience is a source of rest and peace. Dante's often quoted, "In His will is our peace" tells me that doing the will of God brings me peace. It may not bring me personal wealth, fame or fortune, but it will bring me the peace that I too often have tried to find through all those other avenues.

Driving home from work I caught just a snippet of a Crawford Lorrits program on the radio. The series was *Joy: A Resilient Happiness*—"The Source of Joy, Part 2" and was on Psalm 16. What got my attention was when he said obedience to God has two benefits—rest and provision. He talked about how God told the Israelites they were to let the land rest in the seventh year, and that he would make that possible by giving them a double harvest in the sixth year as preparation. It is through our obedience that God makes our future secure (Ps 16:5).

Obedience is God's love language—it is how we show our affection for Him. Again, those who obey His commands grow closer to God and become more like Him.

Obedience advances the cause and work of the church. One of the benefits of obediently making church a part of even your vacations is that sometimes you hear something truly remarkable. I have read and studied the story of Joseph many, many times. But one Sunday some years back when Rod and I were on vacation in Bermuda celebrating our 20th anniversary, I was blessed by a sermon that gave me new insights into Joseph's story. Titled, "Delays on the Way to Destiny", the minister at Cobbs Hill Methodist Church pointed out that when Joseph arrived in Potiphar's house, things were so good for him it must have seemed like the end of the journey after the suffering he endured at the hands of his brothers. But his destiny was far higher and greater, and the way to that destiny required significantly more struggle. The point was not to settle, not to become too complacent with the rest stops on the journey. You can't do that without obedience.

I see from Scripture that obedience is a prerequisite for wisdom: "To obey the Lord is the fundamental principle for wise living; all who carry out his precepts acquire good moral insight. He will receive praise forever." (Psalms 111:10)

And I also read that obedience yields even greater benefits than wisdom. To become what we were created to be is the highest form of joyful obedience.

> The Lord will designate you for himself as a holy people just as he promised you, if you keep his commandments and walk in his ways. (Deuteronomy 28:9)
>
> There will be…glory and honor and peace from God for everyone who does good…for there is no partiality with God. (Romans 2:9-11)
>
> If you have a willing attitude and obey, then you will again eat the good crops of the land. (Isaiah 1:19)

And then there is this wonderful, wonderful reminder that God Himself is working within me, to help me both to *want* what in my own nature I do not want, and to *do* what in my own strength I cannot do. "Continue working out your salvation with awe and reverence, for the one bringing forth in you both the desire and the effort—for the sake of his good pleasure—is God." (Philippians 2:12b, 13)

Who would have thought something so simple as obedience can be of such eternally critical importance? C.S. Lewis in *Mere Christianity* ("The Practical Conclusion" essay) said: "But I wonder whether people who ask God to interfere openly and directly in our world quite realise what it will be like when He does. When that happens, it is the end of the world. When the author walks up on the stage the play is over. God is going to invade, all right; but what is the good of saying you are on His side then, when you see the whole natural universe melting away like a dream and something else—something it never entered your head to conceive—comes crashing in; something so beautiful to some of us and so terrible to others that none of us will have any choice left? For this time it will be God without disguise; something so overwhelming that it will strike either irresistible love or irresistible horror into every creature. There is no use saying you choose to lie down when it has become impossible to stand up. That will not be the time for choosing: it will be the time when we discover which side we really have chosen, whether we realised it before or not."[15]

> [Jesus is speaking] I tell you the solemn truth, if anyone obeys my teaching, he will never see death. (John 8:51)
>
> [Jesus is speaking] If anyone hears my words and does not obey them, I do not judge him. For I have not come to judge the world, but to save the world. The one who rejects me and does not accept my words has a judge; the word I have spoken will judge him at the last day. (John 12:47, 48)
>
> My life is in continual danger, but I do not forget your law. "(Psalms 119:109)

Let me repeat the amazing list of some divine rewards experienced by those who are obedient to God: salvation, eternal life, being filled with the Holy Spirit, true discipleship, wisdom, blessings from God, fulfillment, rest and peace, security, the best life has to offer, restoration of divine innocence, joy, closeness to God, friendship with Jesus.

Why is it that these aren't enough for some of us? It's a question I often wrestle with, especially since I have seen the unexpected rewards of obedience many times in my own life.

- Obedience keeps me from being a recluse. Because the age difference between my older brothers and me was quite large, I grew up essentially an only child. We lived on the outskirts of a tiny coastal town and our only close neighbors were the elderly couple who lived five acres away. Fortunately, I was a voracious reader with an imaginative mind, so I had no trouble entertaining myself. If left alone, even today I am blissfully happy either reading, writing, sewing, or playing chess against the computer. But Jesus Christ calls us to be part of a community, and it is in obedience to Him that I make the effort to reach out and participate in that community—even, or especially, when the experience is awkward or uncomfortable.

- Obedience leads to integrity, which leads to my sleeping well at night. Proverbs 3:27, 28 instructs, "Do not withhold good from those who need it, when you have the ability to do it. Do not say to your neighbor, Go! Return tomorrow and I will give it— when you have it with you at the time." As a small business owner, there have been times when money was so tight I had to choose between paying a vendor or paying myself. The above verse was always the tipping point to my making the right choice. I paid the vendors who were trusting me to pay my bills on time, and I trusted God for the resources I needed in my own life.

- Obedience leads to often surprising reconciliation. In Matthew 5:23, 24, Jesus says, "So then, if you bring your gift to the altar and there remember that your brother has something against you, leave your gift there in front of the altar. First go and be reconciled to your brother and then come and present your gift." I once worked at a job where I had a counterpart named Jim at an outside regulatory agency. Between us we managed a large project that also required the cooperation of several municipalities, whose representatives had a habit of playing us against each other. We had reached a point where our relationship was so contentious, if one of us said the sun rose in the morning, the other would insist it set in the morning. I knew this needed to change. So one day I made an appointment to see Jim, whom I knew to be a genuine Christian. We greeted each other and my first question surprised him: "How much of what you teach in your Sunday School class do you believe?" He blinked and replied, "I like to think I believe all of it." "Even Matthew 5:23, 24?" "Yes. Why?" This was my opening to begin what turned into a creative dialogue about the problems between us and a possible solution, a solution that turned out to be successful. Many years later, I was at a reception after the closing service for a retreat. From across the room, a voice loudly called my name. I turned to see Jim, now an ordained minister, running toward me with a huge smile on his face. After a quick hug, we both burst out laughing. "Who would have imagined we would ever be glad to see each other?" we asked.

Obedience: The Joyful Discipline?

I have many more of these stories, but you get the idea. When we obey God, one of the rewards is having those persistent, pesky wrinkles in our life ironed out!

CHAPTER 9

Heroes of Obedience

In a culture where real heroes—people of unsurpassing character—are becoming increasingly rare, we like to celebrate whatever heroes we can find. Our heroes are most often people who do things we'd like to be able to do if our fears, or what we perceive as our lack of abilities, would allow us to do. We see heroes as having incredible courage, talent, or virtue. We don't see that heroes often don't become heroes until a particular circumstance draws it from them. Mike Burns was the fifth grade classmate who put an end to the merciless bullying I endured; he will forever be a hero to me, even though I doubt he would remember the incident.

You may be a hero in the making and not know it.

It doesn't matter whether heroes are real persons (historical or contemporary) or a work of literary fiction. However, for the purposes of this study I'll leave the fictional heroes—as much as I enjoy reading about them—to someone else to explore. I want to look at some heroes who really lived, heroes who not only believed God but whose actions showed their faith.

Jesus Christ

Jesus Christ is the ultimate hero of joyful obedience.

In one of his sermons, Steve Castle said: "We learn by Jesus' teaching and Jesus' actions what it means to be Christian, who we are called to be as God's children. Jesus was perfectly [and joyfully] obedient."

Our choice is to obey now by choice or be forced to serve later. We must surrender in order to win. Jesus showed active obedience by obeying God's laws and He showed passive obedience when He went to the cross.

Abraham

When we first meet Abraham in the Scriptures, he is Abram, a pagan with no knowledge of God. Yet when the unknown God of the universe called him, Abraham obediently followed the call. Abraham left behind his comfort zone and his larger family and headed out with no idea where the journey would take him. Abraham's obedience ultimately led to our salvation.

Moses

When Moses obeyed God's call to return to Egypt and free the Israelites enslaved to Pharaoh, he showed true heroism. Remember Moses was under a death sentence back in Egypt. When he faced Pharaoh—who was regarded as god incarnate in that culture—and later on Pharaoh's army, Moses did it relying on God's promises and nothing else.

Daniel

Daniel fascinates me. He is one of the few people about whom the Bible records no serious sin (and remember, the Scriptures are quite ready to document the flaws of our ancestors in the faith!). Even his enemies acknowledged that he was, "trustworthy and guilty of no negligence or corruption" (Daniel 6:4).

Taken captive by the Babylonians when just a teenager, Daniel steadfastly refused to be assimilated into that exotic, enticing pagan culture. Even when his determined obedience to worship God and God alone endangered his life, for him there was no question what to do. The last record of him is as an old man, still explaining God and God's purposes to the pagan culture in which he lived and worked.

Peter

Peter is one of my personal favorites. If there was a way to "mess up" on the road to joyful obedience, Peter found it. When given the privilege of seeing the transfigured Jesus Christ, Peter babbled like a fool until God told him to shut up. When the soldiers threatened Jesus, Peter attacked back. After promising Jesus he'd die with Him before he would abandon Him, Peter denied Jesus three times before turning around and to see Jesus looking straight at him. Despite all this, Peter never stopped trying. No matter how badly he fell, he kept getting up and returning to the path of obedience. Peter never quit. I love Peter's example.

Paul

Paul didn't let his past persecution of the early church get in the way of his joyful obedience. By his own description (2 Corinthians 11:23-28), he faced repeated imprisonment, beatings and death. Five times he received 39 lashes, three times he was beaten with a rod, once he was stoned, and three times he was shipwrecked, spending a day and a night adrift on the open sea. He faced dangers from rivers, robbers, his own countrymen, and Gentiles, dangers in the city, in the wilderness, and at sea. He tells of dangers from false brothers, of facing sleepless nights, hunger, thirst, cold, and insufficient clothing. Despite all this, Paul wrote, "Therefore I am content with weaknesses, with insults, with troubles, with persecutions and difficulties for the sake of Christ, for whenever I am weak, then I am strong." (2 Corinthians 12:10)

Mary

Ordinary people become extraordinary people when they obey God. When God chose Mary for one of the most important acts of obedience He has ever asked of anyone, Mary focused on God rather than herself. Her response was simple, unquestioning obedience. Mary put her reputation—indeed, her entire life—on the line when she said "Yes" to God and became the mother of Jesus Christ. Mary was well on her way to living a normal life before the angel Gabriel showed up. Engaged to Joseph and planning her wedding, Mary surely had the usual expectations many young women have of raising a family and living happily ever after. When she told Gabriel, "Yes, I am a servant of the Lord; let this happen to me according to your word." (Luke 1:38), all that changed.

Mary faced disgrace and possibly death when she told Joseph she was pregnant. Even if Joseph pursued neither option, theirs would never be a normal relationship. Her first-born child wasn't his, and apparently that fact was widely known. There were Jews that regarded Jesus as illegitimate and didn't hesitate to say so. Mary really did not receive vindication until after Jesus' resurrection.

And yet, Mary's joy at God's invitation to be the mother of the Messiah was so great that none of this mattered to her. Her joyful obedience, her willingness to do whatever God asked—no matter the personal cost—made our salvation possible.

Zechariah

Although heroes are often revealed in a single significant instant, sometimes heroes are made from the everyday events of living our daily lives. While reading Luke 1:1-25, I noticed that Zechariah received his incredible blessing because he was obedient in his everyday identity as a priest. He is described as righteous in the sight of God, following all the commandments and ordinances of the Lord blamelessly.

Zechariah was obedient to God by being on duty for his appointed week of service at the temple. He didn't call in sick; he didn't find something more important in his own eyes to do that day. He was simply on duty at his regular place of work. And because of that, he received the once in a lifetime opportunity to offer in the holy place the special incense along with prayers for the nation. And as he did so, he saw the first glimmer of that answer to those prayers as well as the answer to the deepest prayer of his and Elizabeth's hearts. It's interesting also that the angel Gabriel tells Zechariah that his coming son will turn the disobedient to the wisdom of the just.

Gideon

Heroes usually show great courage in spite of having great fear. When we first see Gideon in Judges 6:11, he's threshing wheat in the winepress to hide it from the plundering Mideonites. At the angel's greeting, "The Lord is with you, courageous warrior!" Gideon's first response was a scornful, "Pardon me, but if the Lord is with us, why has such disaster overtaken us? Where are all his miraculous deeds our ancestors told us about?" Gideon wasn't afraid to let God know how afraid and uncertain he was. But he obeyed despite his fears.

Joseph

Like Daniel, Joseph fascinates me. Other than his having been a somewhat obnoxious teenager, the Bible records no serious sin committed by Joseph, who apparently had repeated opportunities for doing just that. As the slave in charge of everything Potiphar owned, Joseph could have engaged in larceny and all manner of deceit. He didn't. When Potiphar's amorous wife kept pursuing him, Joseph could resist her advances because his close relationship with God had given him his moral character and convictions long before the seventh commandment was given to Moses. Joseph understood that sin was primarily against God when he asked her, "So how could I do such a great evil, and sin against God"? (Genesis 39:9b)

Hettie Chappell

You have probably never heard of Hettie Chappell. Her name isn't in the Bible, but it's listed in the Lamb's Book of Life. To everyone at St. Peter's United Methodist Church—and much of our community at large—Hettie Chappell was a hero of the first order, someone we all desire to emulate.

In her younger days, Hettie was a nurse who literally loved babies to life. The way she told it to me, the doctors at the hospital often didn't want to fool with sickly newborns and they would sometimes tell the nurses to just ignore these babies so they would die. Hettie Chappell would have none of that. She would defiantly hold and tend these vulnerable babies and love them to full health. I attend church with a woman who was one of those babies.

Hettie Chappell was also a praying woman who loved her Lord. You had the feeling that when Hettie talked, God listened very closely. Every fiber of Hettie's being was oriented towards joyful obedience. When her health was failing in her later years, she leaned unfailingly on the Lord for strength. Whenever you stopped by to visit, she would talk about the goodness of the Lord and pray for you before you left. Hettie even wanted, and got, an altar call incorporated into her funeral service. She wanted to make sure people had every opportunity to join her in heaven.

Oseola McCarty

Oseola McCarty is one of my personal heroes, one of the five people I've never meet with whom I would love to have dinner. I still remember when the news broke about her.

Until almost the end of her life, Oseola McCarty lived in obscurity to everyone except the God she obeyed. Born in Mississippi in 1908, Oseola quit school in the sixth grade to take care of her childless aunt. She became a washerwoman, like her grandmother. Although Oseola's income was counted in nickels, dimes and the occasional quarter, she did three things faithfully and obediently with it: she tithed 10% to her church, she put 10% into a savings account at the bank, and she lived on the rest.

I want you to stop for a moment and think about this. Despite her poverty, Oseola did not neglect her duties to God or herself. She understood how to be content with what she had, even though it was meager by the world's standards. Now, read the rest of this remarkable woman's story.

Since Oseola didn't understand much about money, bank personnel assisted her as her savings grew. When she became older, the bank trust officer asked her to his office. Putting ten dimes on his desk he asked her, if that represented her money, what she would like to be done with it after she passed on. Oseola set aside one dime (10%) for her church and one dime (10%) each for three relatives. She then confided her dream of being able to help someone else get the education she'd never been able to receive, so the remaining six dimes (60%) were allocated to the University of Southern Mississippi. Oseola stipulated that the funds should be used for students, preferably those of African-American descent like herself, who could not otherwise attend college due to financial hardship.

In 1995 Oseola McCarty, an obscure woman with a menial occupation—who had nonetheless obediently handled her meager finances God's way—drew global attention after it was announced she had established a $150,000 trust to provide scholarships for deserving students in need of financial assistance. Did you see that dollar figure? Did you notice how many zeros were in it? Now, please tell me again why you don't make enough money to be obedient with it.

The world acknowledged Oseola McCarty. She was awarded an honorary degree from USM, the first such degree awarded by the university. President Bill Clinton presented her with a Presidential Citizens Medal, the nation's second highest civilian award, during a special White House Ceremony. She won the United Nations' Avicenna Medal for educational commitment. Harvard University awarded McCarty an honorary doctorate.

Even more important, I believe, were the honors that awaited Oseola McCarty when God received her into his kingdom September 26, 1999. I cannot wait to meet her there!

Your Name Here?

You could already be someone's hero and not even know it. Your life, lived in joyful obedience to God, could be all that's missing for someone else to discover the truth of Jesus Christ. Isn't that an exciting opportunity? We all want to live lives that matter. We all want to leave a legacy. What greater meaning can there be than to be significant to another person's life in a way that will impact them for eternity?

The surest way to lose our identity is through disobedience, through behaving the opposite of the way we should. However, through joyful obedience we find out who God created us to be and become that person.

CHAPTER 10

So, What's Your Problem—Besides That?

You may recall the beginning of this book extended an invitation for you to share my exploration of Obedience. I would love to be able to tell you I have now reached the point of perpetual joyful obedience. I haven't. I'm not even close, although I have made significant progress. It is a curious thing, this ebb and flow. Jesus' love is always there, steadfast and true. Through it I have experienced periods of joyful obedience and all its rewards. Yet at times still I struggle, or is it that only now I recognize the struggles?

My most important discovery about obedience has been this: While the road from blind obedience to joyful obedience is straightforward, it is anything but straight. Obedience is a far more nuanced thing than I ever imagined.

When I was in high school, one particular teacher liked to greet students with, "What's your problem today—besides that?" I thought it was a funny, cynical, and (obviously) memorable question. I am asking myself—and you—a version of that same question right now, here at the end of this study on obedience: What's your problem with obedience—besides that?

Go back and review with me the Obstacles to Obedience. Over which one do you keep tripping? I'll admit mine is fear. And yet I know, "There is no fear in love, but perfect love drives out fear, because fear has to do with punishment." (1 John 4:18a) I am keenly aware that Jesus Christ has never, *ever* wounded me. He has proven to be perfectly trustworthy in ways no one else in my life has.

Obedience: The Joyful Discipline?

One question keeps nagging at me: Why isn't God enough? What does God lack that I am still seeking elsewhere? Or is it something else entirely?

Reading a recent newspaper column by noted family psychologist John Rosemond gave me an epiphany. In the column, he pointed out that obedience is not a zero sum game in which the parent wins and the child loses. What an "aha!" moment that was for me! I think that may be the root of our problem with obedience at the highest level. We think if we are obedient, it means God wins and we lose. But in reality, it's the only way we can win.

I think there is also a defensive element to our disobedience. After all, I would rather be rejected for what I do rather than who I am. When I am disobedient, it's about what I *do*. My actions are a smokescreen that forms a protective barrier around me. Or so I tell myself. Actually, disobedience starts inside, in my spirit, and manifests itself in my actions. So I'm only fooling myself to think there is any separation between what I do and who I am. While I may never fully and finally achieve joyful obedience in this earthly life, its pursuit is the best way to fight the destructive influences that are always trying to get my attention.

We've already looked at how active listening leads to truth breaking through. I love the visual imagery of that. Today, when so many people raise their voices to the point of yelling so they can be heard above the other person trying to speak, listening seems a lost art. And, until God's truth breaks through, obedience isn't even on the horizon. It's easier to slip into an imperfect relationship with the world than to pursue a perfect relationship with Jesus Christ through our obedience.

One night at our weekly communion service the reading was from Ephesians 2:1-10. I was captivated by the first part:

> And although you were dead in your transgressions and sins, in which you formerly lived according to this world's present path, according to the ruler of the kingdom of the air, the ruler of the spirit that is now energizing the sons of disobedience, among whom all of us also formerly lived out our lives in the cravings of the flesh, indulging the desires of the flesh and the mind, and were by nature children of wrath even as the rest…But God, being rich in mercy, because of His great love with which He loved us, even though we were dead in transgressions, made us alive together with Christ—by grace you are saved!—and He raised us up with Him and seated us with Him in the heavenly realms in Christ Jesus, to demonstrate in the coming ages the surpassing wealth of His grace in kindness toward us in Christ Jesus. For by grace you are saved through faith, and this is not of yourselves, it is the gift of God; it is not of works, so that no one can boast. For we are His workmanship, having been created in Christ Jesus for good works that God prepared beforehand so we may do them.

Note that although we start out as children of disobedience, we become saved by grace to do good works by the power of Jesus Christ. We *can* learn obedience! We *can* learn to know the Scriptures—which show us the character of God—well enough to live the life we were created to live and we *can* be joyful about, and grateful for, it. I believe having a grateful heart is essential for us to grow into joyful obedience.

If you've ever seen the movie, "The Passion of the Christ", do you remember the last scene? There is the slightest hint of a smile on Jesus' face as He walks out of the tomb. He knows, and because of that, we can also know. His obedience unto death, His obedience learned through suffering, has indeed freed us for joyful obedience.

The music on Easter Sunday is always loud, triumphant and joyful. We need the music of heaven to drown out the voices of this life. We respond to music—it motivates us to dance, to buy, to do things we wouldn't do without it. It can unify us (look at line dancing), it can soothe us (think of David playing the harp for Saul), it can motivate us (i.e., protest music), and it can agitate us (i.e., heavy metal). If we let into our lives the music of heaven—where I believe the stars themselves must sing—joyful obedience becomes a natural response.

It is through the Word that we learn how to be obedient to this God Who never makes mistakes. The God Who created us understands us best and will deal with each of us as He sees best. Unfortunately, all too often we use our God-given uniqueness as the very reason to justify our disobedience. "That doesn't apply to me, my situation is different." "I don't need to do that, it doesn't apply to my personality." "I can't do that, it's just not in my nature." How sad that the very thing that should bring me closer to Him is the very thing I use to run from Him!

One Sunday our District Superintendent, Linda Taylor visited our church and brought the message. She asked us three questions (my spontaneous mental answers follow in brackets):

1. "What is the most important thing for you to know as a Christian? [Jesus loves me and died for my salvation.]
2. What is the most important thing for you to do as a Christian? [Obey God.]
3. Why don't you *do* what you *know*? [Ouch!]

Then she said, "Maybe God loves us even when we don't get it right. Jesus knew the only way to bring perfect people into the kingdom of God is to love them to perfection." Before complaining about someone else's failures in obedience, maybe we should stop and look at how well we are obeying. Is our disobedience a stumbling block to someone else? Jesus had something to say about that:

> Why do you see the speck in your brother's eye, but fail to see the beam of wood in your own? How can you say to your brother, "Brother, let me remove the speck from your eye, while you yourself don't see the beam in your own? You hypocrite! First remove the beam from your own eye, and then you can see clearly to remove the speck from your brother's eye. (Luke 6:41-42)

Remember how the Israelites wanted a rulebook when God wanted joyful obedience? The Bible is indeed a useful rulebook when you first start out on the journey of learning what obedience means. But when you reach the level of joyful obedience you read the Bible differently. You start reading it as a love story, understanding what it means to live in relationship with the living God. You understand how completely trustworthy our God is:

> God is not a man that he should lie, nor the son of man, that he should repent. Has he said, and will he not do it? Or has he spoken, and will he not establish it? (Numbers 23:19)

> In the same way God wanted to demonstrate more clearly to the heirs of the promise that his purpose was unchangeable, and so he intervened with an oath, so that we who have found refuge in him may find strong

> encouragement to hold fast to the hope set
> before us through two unchangeable things,
> since it is impossible for God to lie. (Hebrews
> 6:17, 18)

Karl Zorowski gave a thoughtful sermon titled, "What Have You Done with My Penguins?" In it he said, "Joyful obedience means no longer reacting to an order or expectation, but it's a way of living a life described by God's laws. The Bible is not a history book, it's not fiction; it is the means through which God can reveal Himself to us in an ongoing presence."

I experienced the joyful obedience Karl described while working on this book. Someone important to me had deeply hurt my feelings. This person made a thoughtless, minimizing comment about me to someone else *while I was standing there with them*! I was angry and later—in private—I talked to the person about it, only to be put down again. That left me angrier. Actually, I was seething inside. While I was focusing on my resentment, suddenly and most unexpectedly Proverbs 19:11 starting running through my head, over and over and over again: "A person's wisdom makes him slow to anger, and it is his glory to overlook an offense." Slowly it dawned on me that this is the only place in the entire Bible where God tells us we can do something that is to *our* glory, not just His! As I meditated on the verse, I made a conscious decision to overlook the offense and let it go. It was a truly, completely joy-filled experience.

Allow me to close with a final thought. Have you ever had the opportunity to meet a celebrity or one of your personal heroes? It was very exciting, wasn't it? One of my good friends once took a group of youth cross-country to see the Pope. He said the excitement as they stood in the stands, waiting for the Pope to appear, was almost unbearable. Then, as he was craning his neck straining for the first glimpse of the Pope, he heard the Lord ask, "Are you looking for My coming with this much excitement and anticipation?"

The God of the universe is greater than any and all of our earthly heroes, and He is waiting to have a close personal relationship with you. Our proper response to God's grace is joyful obedience. And it *is* possible.

What's stopping you?

End Notes

Introduction

1. *The United Methodist Hymnal* © The United Methodist Publishing House, Nashville, TN.
2. "My Spiritual Vocabulary", Debbie Macomber, www.guideposts.org/stories-of-faith/choosingwordstoliveby.

Defining Obedience

3. *Webster's Third New International Dictionary*, 3rd ed., G&C Miriam Co., 1966.
4. *Mere Christianity* by C.S. Lewis copyright© C.S. Lewis Pte. Ltd. 1942,1943,1944,1952.

More Than a Definition

5. *That Hideous Strength* by C.S. Lewis copyright© C.S. Lewis Pte. Ltd. 1945.

Whom Do You Obey?

6. *Mere Christianity* by C.S. Lewis copyright© C.S. Lewis Pte. Ltd. 1942,1943,1944,1952.
7. Tim Challies, "Counterfeit Detection" (Part 1) June 27, 2006. www.challies.com/articles/counterfeit-detection-part-1.

How Do You Obey?

8. *The Screwtape Letters* by C.S. Lewis copyright© C.S. Lewis Pte. Ltd. 1942.

It Isn't Easy (Obstacles to Obedience)

9. *Mere Christianity* by C.S. Lewis copyright© C.S. Lewis Pte. Ltd. 1942,1943,1944,1952.
10. *Surprised by Joy* by C.S. Lewis copyright© C.S. Lewis Pte. Ltd. 1955.
11. *Mere Christianity* by C.S. Lewis copyright© C.S. Lewis Pte. Ltd. 1942,1943,1944,1952.
12. *Mere Christianity* by C.S. Lewis copyright© C.S. Lewis Pte. Ltd. 1942,1943,1944,1952.
13. *Mere Christianity* by C.S. Lewis copyright© C.S. Lewis Pte. Ltd. 1942,1943,1944,1952.

The Divine Rewards of Obedience

14. *The Last Battle* by C.S. Lewis copyright© C.S. Lewis Pte. Ltd. 1956
15. *Mere Christianity* by C.S. Lewis copyright© C.S. Lewis Pte. Ltd. 1942,1943,1944,1952.

www.ingramcontent.com/pod-product-compliance
Lightning Source LLC
LaVergne TN
LVHW051520070426
835507LV00023B/3214